Contents

Acknowledgements

The authors and publishers are grateful to the kind assistance of David Hartley, Mike Chapple and John Warren for their painstaking work in reading and commenting on the manuscripts.

The authors and publishers are grateful to the following for permission to reproduce copyright photographs.

Allsport: Part title, page 7 (Simon Bruty), Figure 16.8 (Bernard Asset/Vandystadt), Figure 22.6

Images Colour Library: Figures 15.3, 20.5

Image Select: Figures 1.2, 6.1, 7.4, 10.7 (all NASA), Figure 22.5 (J.-M. Loubat)

Science Photo Library: Half title page (Roger Ressmeyer), Figures 1.1 (Michael Gilbert), 5.1 (Mehau Kulyk), 9.6 (US Library of Congress), 12.9 (Philippe Plailly), 16.3 (Prof. Harold Egerton), 16.5 (Rev. Ronald Royer), 22.7 (NASA), 16.10 (European Space Agency)

Alan Thomas: Figures 1.3, 1.4, 1.6, 2.5, 2.6, 2.8, 3.1, 3.6, 24.4, 27.3, 32.2, 37.7

Andy Ross Photography: Figures 2.7, 6.2, 23.5, 24.1, 24.6, 25.1, 25.2, 25.3, 25.4, 25.5, 25.6, 29.2, 35.1, 35.5

The authors and publishers are grateful to the following for permission to reproduce copyright photographs.Simon Bell

Nelson Advanced Modular Science

Mechanics and Electricity

MARK ELLSE • CHRIS HONEYWILL

Thomas Nelson UK
Nelson House Mayfield Road
Walton-on-Thames Surrey
KT12 5PL UK

© Mark Ellse, Chris Honeywill 1997

First published by Thomas Nelson and Sons Ltd 1997

I(T)P Thomas Nelson is an International Thomson Publishing Company
I(T)P is used under licence

ISBN 0-17-448260-4
NPN 9 8 7 6 5 4 3 2 1

Printed in Spain

Publishing team:
Acquisitions: Mary Ashby/Chris Coyer
Administration: Jenny Goode
Staff editorial: Simon Bell
Freelance editorial: Geoff Amor/Theresa Brady
Marketing: Jane Lewis
Production: Liam Reardon
Staff design: Maria Pritchard
Design/Typesetting: Pentacor plc

Preface

This book takes you through the first Module of the Edexcel London Examinations A-level and AS-level Physics syllabus. It is also suitable for the core content of other A-level schemes. We have divided the book into small chapters, each of which introduces only a few new ideas.

Within the chapters are suggestions for experiments. You may not do or see all the experiments, but you should think about them as you read the text and try to predict what the experiments would show. Most of the experiments are described in a way that you could use yourself as an answer to an examination question that required an experimental description.

Important terms are highlighted in **bold**. There is a list of these terms, under the heading 'Things you need to know' on pages 124–127 of this book.

On pages 110–118 you will find practice questions to try after studying each chapter. There is also a selection of past examination questions.

The chapters are in a possible teaching order, but as far as possible we have tried to make them self-contained so that you can use them in any order, or dip into them for revision.

This book is one of a series of four Module texts for Edexcel London Examinations A-level Physics.

Alongside them is published a set of Experiment Sheets by Adrian Watt which describe in greater detail how to carry out many of the experiments in the texts. There is also a Teacher's Guide, showing how the different publications relate to the examination syllabus and giving guidance on apparatus.

Mark Ellse is Managing Director of Chase Academy, Cannock, Staffordshire and a Principal Examiner for Edexcel London Examinations.

Chris Honeywill is Deputy Registrar and former Head of Physics at The Sixth Form College, Farnborough, Hampshire, and an Assistant Principal Examiner for Edexcel London Examinations.

Physics:

The science of measurement

Measuring the distance to the Moon by sending a laser beam through a telescope and back

1 The International System of Units

Physical quantities

Figure 1.1   Part of an atom

From smaller than the nucleus of the atom (Figure 1.1) to the giant scale of galaxies (Figure 1.2); from events that take place faster than a billionth of a second to the age of the universe: measurement is central to the study of physics.

In your study of physics you will measure a range of quantities, from such obvious ones as distance and time to more subtle ones like magnetic flux density and capacitance. All these things that physicists measure are called **physical quantities**.

When studying part of an atom, you might be interested in the quantities mass and diameter. When studying a star, you might want to know about the quantities temperature and age. In an electrical circuit, you will want to know about the quantities current, voltage and resistance.

Derived and base quantities

Many physical quantities are combinations of others. These are **derived quantities**. For example, a volume is the product of three lengths, while speed is a length divided by a time. But in any system of units you have to start from somewhere. These starting quantities are **base quantities**. By international agreement there are seven base quantities. You will use only six of them in your A-level course. These are mass, length, time, current, amount of substance and temperature interval. (The seventh base quantity is luminous intensity.) All other quantities are derived from these base quantities.

Figure 1.2   A distant galaxy

Figure 1.3   The mass of an adult is about 70 kg

Units

If you want to compare your own measurements with others, you need to take measurements in the same way and use the same agreed size or magnitude of quantity for measurement. The agreed magnitudes are called **units** and there are standard units for the whole range of physical quantities.

For measuring the quantity length, the agreed magnitude for comparison (the unit) is the metre. For time, the unit is the second. You may be familiar with the amp and the ohm as units of current and resistance, but may be less familiar with the tesla and the farad as units of magnetic field strength and capacitance.

Base and derived units

The units for the base quantities are defined without reference to any other units. These are base units. The International System of Units, abbreviated to SI (from the French *Système International*), agrees base units for the base quantities. In Britain, the National Physical Laboratory works with other laboratories overseas to make sure that base units that are used in one place are the same as those used elsewhere, so that, for instance, the kilogram used on one balance is the same as the kilogram used on any other.

Table 1.1 on page 4 lists the base units along with their symbols. Most base units are defined in a way that can be reproduced anywhere in the world, but the kilogram is, rather inconveniently, defined by a standard kilogram (called the prototype kilogram) kept in Paris. This means that all other kilogram masses must be compared, directly or indirectly, with the prototype.

Derived units are defined with reference to the base units. The unit of force, the newton, is a derived unit. It is defined from the base units kilogram, metre and second.

Figure 1.4   The current through this lamp is about a quarter of an amp

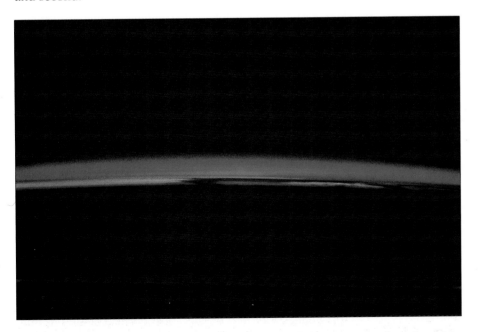

Figure 1.5   The average temperature of the Earth is about 300K, and that of the surface of the Sun is about 5000K

Table 1.1 *Base quantities and units*

Base quantity	Base unit	Symbol	Definition
length	metre	m	the distance that an electromagnetic wave travels in a time of 1/299 792 458 second
mass	kilogram	kg	the mass equal to that of the standard kilogram
time	second	s	9 192 631 770 oscillations of a caesium atomic clock
current	ampere	A	that constant current which, when it is flowing in two infinitely long parallel thin wires that are 1 m apart in vacuum, produces between them a force per unit length of $2 \times 10^{-7} \, N\,m^{-1}$
temperature interval	kelvin	K	1/273.16 of the thermodynamic temperature of the triple point of water
amount of substance	mole	mol	the amount of substance that contains as many elementary units as there are atoms in 12 g of carbon-12

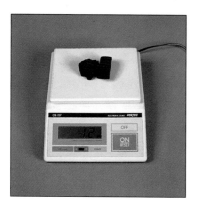

Figure 1.6 Twelve grams of carbon contain one mole of atoms

Comparing quantities

You express physical measurements as multiples of a physical unit. For instance, a race track might be 100 metres long—100 times as long as the metre, the standard unit for length. A girl's mass might be 55 kilograms—55 times as large as the mass standard, the kilogram. All measurements are expressed like this, as a number multiplied by a unit. Larger and smaller multiples can be written with prefixes (Table 1.2). The measurement is the *product* of a number and a unit. You need to include both the number and the unit when stating the result of a measurement. If you leave either out then the statement is meaningless. Figures 1.3 to 1.6 show some examples.

Word equations

Derived quantities and their units are defined by word equations. For example, the derived quantity speed is defined in terms of the two base quantities distance and time by the equation

$$\text{speed} = \frac{\text{distance}}{\text{time}}$$

All derived quantities are built up from base quantities by a series of word equations. You can use an equation with symbols instead of a word equation if you state the meaning of the symbols. For example, $v = x/t$, where v is speed and x is distance covered in time t.

The word equation that defines a derived physical quantity also defines its unit. For example, the units of distance and time are metres and seconds, so the unit of speed is the metre per second.

Homogeneity

An equation which states that two things are equal only makes sense if those two things are of the same type. It makes sense to say

$$5 \text{ kg} = 3 \text{ kg} + 2 \text{ kg}$$

but no sense at all to say

$$5 \text{ kg} = 3 \text{ kg} + 2 \text{ m} \quad \text{or} \quad 5 \text{ kg} = 5 \text{ ms}^{-1}$$

Even though the numbers are equal, the units show that the quantities are not of the same type.

Quantities that you say are equal, or that you add together must be of the same type. The word **homogeneous**, from Greek, means *same type*. A physical equation can only be correct if it equates or adds together homogeneous quantities.

Correct equations must be homogeneous but homogeneous equations are not automatically correct. Even if the units are equivalent, the numbers may not be correct. The equations

$$5 \text{ kg} = 3 \text{ kg} + 1 \text{ kg} \quad \text{or} \quad \text{speed} = 6 \times \frac{\text{distance}}{\text{time}}$$

are both homogeneous, but clearly incorrect.

Table 1.2 *You can use prefixes with units to express larger or smaller multiples*

Prefix	Symbol	Multiplier
giga	G	10^9
mega	M	10^6
kilo	k	10^3
milli	m	10^{-3}
micro	μ	10^{-6}
nano	n	10^{-9}
pico	p	10^{-12}

Table 1.3 *Some typical magnitudes*

	Length/m	Mass/g	Time/s	Current/A	Temperature/K	Amount of substance/mol
pico (10^{-12})	wavelength of a gamma ray	10^{12} protons	period of molecular spin	current when 6×10^6 electrons pass a point in one second		10^{10} units
nano (10^{-9})	length of a molecule of olive oil	speck of dust	very fast computer switch time	ionisation current caused by a match flame		amount of carbon in this full stop.
micro (10^{-6})	typical size of a bacterium	small grain of sand	period of a radio wave	current drawn by a digital watch	about as cold as you can get	grain of salt
milli (10^{-3})	diameter of a pinhead	raindrop	period of a sound wave	current through 1.5 kΩ resistor connected to a dry cell		carbon dioxide exhaled during one breath
reference unit	height of a laboratory bench	smallest mammal	tick of a grandfather clock	current drawn by a car headlamp	cosmic background temperature	2g of hydrogen gas
kilo (10^3)	Big Ben to Nelson's column	1 litre of milk	mean lifetime of a free neutron	current drawn by a 'Chunnel' train	melting point of silver	bucketful of water
mega (10^6)	Land's End to John O'Groats	1 m³ of water	11 days	current drawn by all the houses in a large town	outermost atmosphere of the sun	your annual consumption of water
giga (10^9)	diameter of the sun	large tree from a rainforest	duration of the Thirty Years' War	current drawn by all the towns in Britain	core of the hottest stars	oxygen inhaled during a lifetime

Mechanics

An example of 120kg moving at 10ms^{-1}

2 Displacement, velocity and acceleration

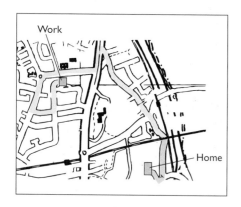

Figure 2.1 *Though the distance travelled from home to work is 4km, the displacement from home is never as much as 2km*

Distance and displacement

The study of motion is called kinematics. The easiest thing to measure about motion is how far something moves, the distance it travels.

If you walk 4 km from home to work, and 4 km back from work to home, then you have travelled a total distance of 8 km, assuming that you sit still all day. On the other hand, by the end of the day you are back where you started, so you end up no distance at all from your starting point. If your route to work has corners and bends, you will never be as much as 4 km from your home. Distance to work alone does not give you information about how far, directly, is the distance from home to work. Nor does distance indicate the direction from home to work.

There is another quantity that states both the magnitude and direction of a change in position. It is called **displacement** – the distance moved in a particular direction. If your route to work is like that in Figure 2.1, your displacement during the day is about 2 km north-west. Half-way between home and work, the displacement is still about 2 km, but in a different direction; when you get back home at night, your displacement is zero.

Vectors and scalars

Distance and displacement are examples of two different types of quantities: **scalars** and **vectors**. Scalar quantities have size (magnitude) only and no direction. All the base quantities are scalar quantities and, like distance, have no direction.

Vector quantities have both size and direction. Displacement has both size and direction, and is a vector quantity. Other examples of vector quantities are force, velocity and acceleration.

Adding scalars and vectors

You can add scalars by simple arithmetic. A distance of 5 km followed by another distance of 5 km gives a total distance of 10 km. But when adding a vector like displacement you must take into account the direction. Remember that 4 km to work and then 4 km back gives a total displacement of zero rather than 8 km.

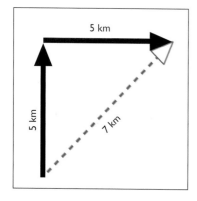

Figure 2.2 *The resultant of these two displacements is just over 7km north-east*

If you have a displacement of 5 km north and then a displacement of 5 km east, you end up north-east of your starting point, as Figure 2.2 shows. You can find the final displacement (called the resultant displacement) by drawing a diagram to represent the displacements in turn. If you draw the diagram to scale, you can take measurements from the diagram to find the final displacement. Or, you can draw a sketch diagram and calculate the resultant mathematically. In this case the resultant displacement is just over 7 km north-east of the starting point.

Any vectors can be added like this, representing them in size and direction by lines on a diagram and then calculating their resultant, or measuring it from the diagram.

Speed

Speed is distance moved per second. You find it by measuring the time to travel a known distance and then dividing the distance by the time. That is,

$$\text{speed} = \frac{\text{distance}}{\text{time}}$$

In many situations, the speed of an object is changing. For example, a sprinter (Figure 2.3) starts slowly and quickly gathers speed. The **average speed**, as its name implies, averages all the different speeds:

$$\text{average speed} = \frac{\text{total distance travelled}}{\text{total time taken}}$$

Both speed and average speed are scalar quantities; direction is not relevant.

Velocity

Just as displacement is the vector that corresponds to distance, **velocity** is the vector that corresponds to speed:

$$\text{velocity} = \frac{\text{displacement}}{\text{time}}$$

As with displacement, strictly you should give the direction of any velocity. A car that is travelling northwards along a road at a *speed* of 30 m s^{-1} has a *velocity* of 30 m s^{-1} *northwards*.

A car moving along a road at a steady speed changes direction as the road bends. Though its speed is constant, its direction of motion is not; so the velocity is changing as it travels around the bend.

Many kinematics problems concern linear motion in which objects move only in straight lines. In these the direction is often obvious and you do not need to specify it all the time. But objects moving in a straight line go backwards as well as forwards, so you do need to specify one direction as positive, and use positive and negative signs to show direction.

Adding velocities

The instruments on an aircraft indicate the velocity of the aircraft relative to the air it flies through. But the air through which it flies moves relative to the ground. If the pilots wish to know the aircraft's velocity relative to the ground, they, or their computers, need to add the velocity of the aircraft relative to the air to the velocity of the air relative to the ground.

Figure 2.4 shows an aircraft flying west, at 150 m s^{-1} relative to the air, at the same time as a wind is blowing at 40 m s^{-1} from the north-west relative to the ground. You add the two velocities in just the same way as displacements. The resultant velocity is 125 m s^{-1} at an angle of 13° south of west.

Figure 2.3   A sprinter increases her/his speed quickly over the first few metres

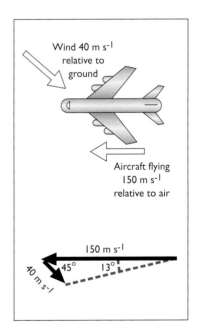

Figure 2.4   The velocity of the aircraft relative to the ground is the sum of its velocity relative to the air, plus the velocity of the air relative to the ground

Measuring velocity

- Set up a sloping runway and measure its length. Release the trolley from the top and time how long it takes to run to the bottom.
- Calculate the average velocity.
- Repeat your measurements and calculations a few times to check that they are reliable.
- Put a card of measured length on top of the trolley and use a timer to measure how long the card takes to pass through a light beam. (Figure 2.5)
- Measure the velocity of the trolley like this near the top of the runway and near the bottom of the runway. (You may have an intelligent timer that does the calculations for you.)
- Compare these velocities with the average velocity down the runway.

Figure 2.5   Trolley with card interrupter

Average velocity and instantaneous velocity

The average velocity is the total displacement divided by the total time. If the velocity is changing, the velocity at any instant, called the instantaneous velocity, is different from the average velocity. To find the instantaneous velocity, you need to measure the change in displacement over a very tiny time interval, and divide that displacement by the short time.

Acceleration

When the velocity of any object changes, the object is accelerating. The trolley in the above experiment is accelerating. The **acceleration** is the quantity that indicates how fast the velocity is changing. It is the change in velocity per second:

$$\text{acceleration} = \frac{\text{change in velocity}}{\text{time taken for change}}$$

If the trolley starts at rest, and 2 s later has a speed of 1.8 m s^{-1}, then

$$\text{acceleration} = \frac{\text{change in velocity}}{\text{time taken for change}} = \frac{(1.8 \text{ m s}^{-1} - 0 \text{ m s}^{-1})}{2 \text{ s}} = 0.9 \text{ m s}^{-2}$$

As the calculation shows, the units of acceleration are m s^{-2}.

The size of the acceleration indicates how much the velocity changes every second. The trolley starts at rest. One second later its velocity is 0.9 m s^{-1}. Two seconds after starting, its velocity is 1.8 m s^{-1}. What will the velocity be 3 s after starting if the acceleration continues at the same rate?

Acceleration is a vector quantity; direction is important. If you measure displacement down the slope as positive, the trolley on the runway has a positive acceleration; the acceleration causes the velocity down the slope to increase.

Measuring acceleration

- Set up a sloping runway. Fix two cards of the same known length onto the trolley so that they interrupt the light beam twice as the trolley rolls down (Figure 2.6). Let the trolley roll; use an intelligent timer to measure the time of the two interruptions and the time between them.
- Calculate the average velocity of the trolley during each interruption.
- Divide the change in velocity by the time taken for the change, to find the acceleration.
- Drop a double interrupter card through a light gate connected to a timer to measure the acceleration of the falling card (Figure 2.7). What value do you get?
- Add masses to the card and repeat your measurements.

Figure 2.6   Trolley with double interrupter

Figure 2.7   A double interrupter card dropping through a light gate

Rate of change

Rate of means 'divided by time'. So rate of change of displacement means change in displacement divided by time, which is velocity. Rate of change of velocity means change in velocity divided by time, which is acceleration.

Using ticker timers and video cameras to measure acceleration

- A ticker timer puts 50 ticks on a tape per second. Let the trolley pull a tape through the ticker timer as it runs down the runway (Figure 2.8).
- Calculate the average velocity at 0.1 s intervals (Figure 2.9) and plot a graph of velocity against time to calculate the acceleration.
- A video camera takes 25 pictures per second. Video your trolley running down the runway, with a calibrated scale in the background. Play the video back a frame at a time and measure from the screen the distance travelled per frame.
- Compare these results with those using the ticker timer.

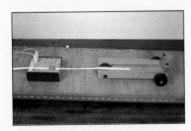

Figure 2.8   Trolley with ticker timer

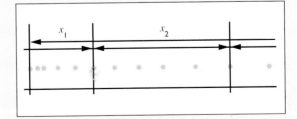

Figure 2.9   Mark the start of the tape (first tick) and tabulate values of the distance every five ticks afterwards. This is the distance covered each tenth of a second

3 Motion graphs

Measuring displacement

- A motion sensor sends out a pulse of ultrasound waves and times how long the pulse takes to return, so it can determine how far away an object is.
- Set up the motion sensor at the top of a runway. Use it to measure how far away from it the trolley is (Figure 3.1). Check its measurements with a ruler.
- Let the trolley run down the slope and use the sensor and computer to plot a graph to show how the displacement changes with time.
- Repeat for a range of different slopes.

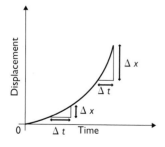

Figure 3.1   A motion sensor can measure distance to the trolley

Figure 3.2   The slope of a displacement–time graph is the velocity

Displacement–time graphs

Figure 3.2 shows how the displacement varies with time for the trolley running down the runway. At the beginning, the graph is shallow; at the end it is steeper. The mathematical quantity which measures the steepness of the graph is the gradient. When the graph is a curve, the gradient is changing. You calculate the gradient of any graph by using the formula

$$\text{gradient} = \frac{\text{change in vertical step}}{\text{corresponding change in horizontal step}}$$

For the graph in Figure 3.2, the total change in the vertical step is equal to the total displacement and the total change in horizontal step is equal to the time for that displacement. So

$$\text{gradient of the dotted line} = \frac{\text{total displacement}}{\text{time for that displacement}} = \text{average velocity}$$

The gradient at any point on the graph is equal to the tiny change in vertical step divided by the corresponding horizontal step. The **gradient of a displacement–time graph** at any point is the instantaneous velocity at that point. As Figure 3.3 shows, the instantaneous velocity of the trolley increases as it runs down the slope.

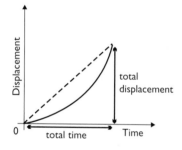

Figure 3.3   The instantaneous velocity at two points

The symbol Δx is used to represent the small displacements used to calculate the slope, and the corresponding times are indicated by the symbol Δt. The velocity is $\Delta x/\Delta t$. (The Greek letter delta Δ is used to indicate that the changes are very small.) The quantity $\Delta x/\Delta t$ at any point is equal to the gradient at that point and is therefore the instantaneous velocity.

By seeing how the slope of a displacement–time graph changes, you can produce a velocity–time graph. Figure 3.4 shows the displacement–time and velocity–time graphs for a trolley running down a runway.

Velocity–time graphs

A trolley running down a slope starts off at rest and its velocity increases by the same amount every second. The velocity–time graph is a straight line through the origin. The **gradient of a velocity–time graph** is the change in velocity divided by the time for that change. This is the acceleration.

For this graph, the gradient, and therefore the acceleration, is $\Delta v/\Delta t$, where Δv is the change in velocity and Δt is the time taken for that change. (Again the letter Δ is used to indicate that the changes are small.)

For the trolley running down the slope, the velocity–time graph is a straight line. Its gradient is constant, showing that the acceleration is constant, as shown by Figure 3.4.

Area under a velocity–time graph

Figure 3.5 shows a velocity–time graph. The area under the graph for the small time Δt is shaded. Since the strip is narrow, the average velocity is approximately the same as v, the velocity at the midpoint of the narrow strip. The area of the strip is $v\Delta t$, which is also equal to the average velocity multiplied by the time. This is the change of displacement in time Δt.

The same is true for all the rest of the strips that make up the area under the graph. So the final displacement is the total area underneath the graph. For any velocity–time graph, the **area under a velocity–time graph** is equal to the displacement.

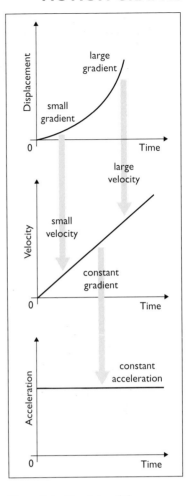

Figure 3.4   *The slope of the displacement–time graph is the velocity, and the slope of the velocity–time graph is the acceleration*

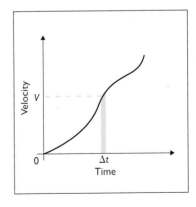

Figure 3.5   *The shaded area under the velocity–time graph is equal to the displacement during time Δt*

Bouncing ball

- Use the motion sensor to produce displacement–time, velocity–time and acceleration–time graphs for a bouncing ball (Figure 3.6).

Figure 3.6 Set up the motion sensor above the bouncing ball

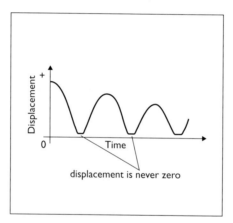

Figure 3.7 Displacement–time graph of the centre of a bouncing ball above the ground

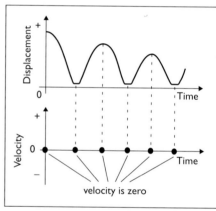

Figure 3.8 The velocity is zero where the gradient is zero

Sketching kinematics graphs

The displacement–time graph for a bouncing ball looks familiar enough (Figure 3.7). But the situation is complicated, and a good one in which to practise the skill of sketching velocity–time and acceleration–time graphs from a displacement–time graph. Figures 3.7 to 3.12 guide you through this process.

Notice that the displacement is never zero (Figure 3.7), because the centre of the ball never touches the ground. The velocity is zero where the gradient of the displacement–time graph is zero. First mark these points (Figure 3.8). At points like A (Figure 3.9), the gradient of the displacement–time graph is large and positive; so is the velocity. At points like B, the slope of the displacement–time graph is large and negative; so is the velocity.

When the ball is in contact with the ground (Figure 3.10), ie during the brief bounces, the gradient changes rapidly from negative to positive; so does the velocity.

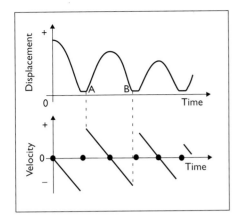

Figure 3.9   The velocity is large and positive at points like A, and large and negative at points like B

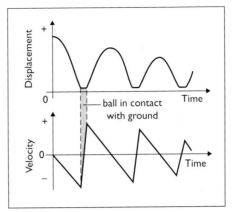

Figure 3.10   When the ball is in contact with the ground, the velocity changes rapidly

While the ball is in the air (Figure 3.11), the gradient of the velocity–time graph is constant and negative; so is the acceleration. The acceleration is constant, because it is equal to the acceleration of gravity. The acceleration is negative because it is downwards and we are using a sign convention that says upwards is positive.

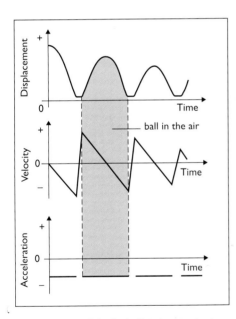

Figure 3.11   While the ball is in the air, the acceleration is constant and negative

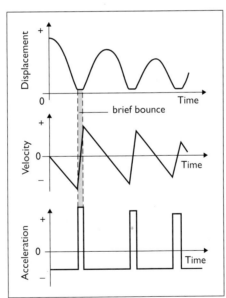

Figure 3.12   During the brief bounces, the acceleration is large and positive

During the brief bounces (Figure 3.12), the velocity changes a large amount from negative to positive as the ball changes direction. This is a large positive change of velocity in a short time. The large and positive acceleration is caused by the force of the ground on the ball. The gradient of the velocity–time graph is constant, large and positive; so is the acceleration. It is greater than the downwards acceleration of gravity.

4 Equations of motion

Table 4.1 *Symbols used in kinematics equations*

v	final velocity	m s^{-1}
u	initial velocity	m s^{-1}
$x\ s$	displacement	m
a	acceleration	m s^{-2}
t	time	s

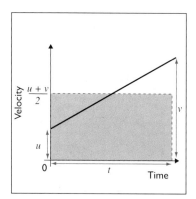

Figure 4.1   Average velocity is $(u + v)/2$

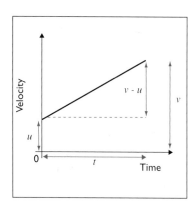

Figure 4.2   Final velocity is $v = u + (v - u) = u + at$

The need for equations

Kinematics equations give a mathematical picture of a moving object. They allow you to make calculations about the motion of the object. This chapter introduces equations which describe the motion of an object moving with constant acceleration in a straight line, the most common situation that you will encounter. The chapter shows where the equations come from, but the important thing is that you know how to apply them.

Table 4.1 shows the symbols and the units used for final and initial velocities, displacement, acceleration and time.

Average velocity equation

You know that:

$$\text{average velocity} = \frac{\text{displacement}}{\text{time taken}}$$

If a body has a constant acceleration, you can find the average velocity by adding together the initial and final velocities and dividing by 2. So:

$$\text{average velocity} = \frac{(u + v)}{2} = \frac{x}{t} \quad \text{Rearranging,} \quad x = \frac{(u + v)}{2} t$$

This is shown in Figure 4.1.

$$S = ut + \tfrac{1}{2}at^2$$

Acceleration equation

The word equation for acceleration is used to derive this equation:

$$\text{acceleration} = \frac{\text{change in velocity}}{\text{time for change}}$$

Since change in velocity = final velocity − initial velocity you can write

$$a = \frac{(v - u)}{t} \quad \text{giving} \quad at = v - u$$

so $v = u + at$
This is shown in Figure 4.2.

Displacement equation

Displacement is equal to the area under a velocity–time graph. Figure 4.3 shows a body with initial velocity u. It accelerates at a constant rate to velocity v in a time t. The body's displacement is the area under the graph; it is split up into a rectangle and a triangle.

The rectangle has height u and length t. Its area is therefore equal to ut. The triangle also has a base length t. Its height is $v-u$ and from the acceleration equation, we know that $v-u = at$. We therefore have a triangle of base t and height at. The area of this is $\frac{1}{2}at^2$. So

$$\begin{aligned} \text{displacement} &= \text{total area under graph} \\ &= \text{area of rectangle} + \text{area of triangle} \\ x &= ut + \tfrac{1}{2}at^2 \end{aligned}$$

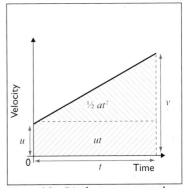

Figure 4.3 *Displacement x equals the area under a velocity–time graph, that is, $x = ut + \frac{1}{2}at^2$*

The fourth equation

You can combine two of the above equations to make another useful equation which leaves out the quantity time. First rearrange $v = u + at$ to give an equation for t:

$$t = \frac{(v-u)}{a}$$

Then substitute this into the equation

$$x = \frac{(u+v)}{2}t$$

This gives

$$x = \frac{(u+v)}{2}\frac{(v-u)}{a}$$

$$x = \frac{(u+v)(v-u)}{2a}$$

$$2ax = (u+v)(v-u)$$

$$2ax = v^2 - u^2$$

$$v^2 = u^2 + 2ax$$

Some tips for solving kinematics problems

1 Be careful and methodical in your physics calculations:
2 Remember that kinematics equations apply only when (i) the acceleration is constant, (ii) the motion is in a straight line and (iii) the displacement x is 0 when the time t is 0.
3 Say '*vuxat*' and make a little table of the quantities showing what you know and what you need to find out. Remember that 'starting from rest' means that $u = 0$.
4 Convert the units to a coherent set, usually metres and seconds.
5 Choose your equation to contain the quantity you need and those that you know.
6 Substitute, rearrange and calculate.
7 Remember the unit in your answer.

Worked example

A sprinter starts from rest and reaches a speed of 10 m s^{-1} after covering a distance of 500 cm. Calculate the acceleration, assuming that this is constant.

We have

$v = 10$ m s^{-1}

$u = 0$ since starting from rest

$x = 500$ cm $= 5$ m

$a = ?$ (m s^{-2}) you have to find this

$t =$ (not needed)

The only equation which contains these four quantities is

$v^2 = u^2 + 2ax$

Numerically,

$10^2 = 0^2 + 2 \times a \times 5$

$100 = 10a$

$a = 10$ m s^{-2}

5 Falling under gravity

Equal acceleration

Chapter 2 described how to measure acceleration by timing two interruptions of a light gate, by using ticker tape, and by videoing an accelerating object. If you use these methods to measure the acceleration of a range of falling bodies, you find that for most bodies the acceleration is the same. Of course, in air, a very light body like a feather has less acceleration than a denser body like a hammer. But when both fall freely through a vacuum, it is easy to demonstrate that they have the same acceleration (Figure 5.1). This is the acceleration due to gravity, known as g.

For most objects falling through a few metres, from cannon balls to tennis balls, air resistance has little effect and their acceleration in air is constant and equal to g.

Figure 5.1   The hammer and feather experiment

Timing a falling ball

- The electromagnet holds the steel ball when the switch is in position A in Figure 5.2.
- Measure the distance x from the bottom of the ball to the top of the trapdoor.
- Switch to position B. The electromagnet releases the ball, the clock circuit is completed and the clock starts.
- When the ball hits the trapdoor, it opens the clock circuit and the clock stops. Record the time t for the ball to fall.
- Repeat and measure the time twice more. Average the three values.
- Repeat for a range of different heights.
- Plot a graph of x against t^2.

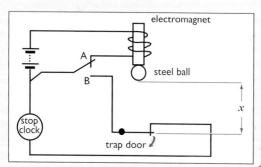

Figure 5.2   Diagram showing circuit for accurate timing of a falling ball

Calculating *g* from the time taken to fall a known distance

Air resistance hardly affects the acceleration of a falling steel ball, so its acceleration is very close to that due to gravity.

The ball falls a distance *x* from rest in a time *t*. The acceleration can then be found from the equation

$$x = ut + \tfrac{1}{2}at^2$$

Since $u = 0$, and the acceleration $a = g$:

$$x = \tfrac{1}{2}gt^2$$

Rearranging:

$$g = \frac{2x}{t^2}$$

If you measure *x* and *t*, you can use this equation to calculate a single value for the acceleration.

A better method for measuring *g* is to make a series of measurements of the time *t* taken to fall a range of distances *x*. Compare the equation

$$x = \tfrac{1}{2}gt^2$$

with

$$y = mx + c$$

which is the equation for a straight line with gradient *m* and intercept *c* on the *y* axis. If you plot a graph of *x* against t^2, its gradient will be $\tfrac{1}{2}g$. The constant *c* will be zero, showing that the graph will go through the origin. You can measure the gradient of your graph and double it to find *g*.

Vertical projection

Projection simply means throwing. If you project an object into the air, its acceleration after you have let it go is always downwards, whether it is on the way up, at the top, or on the way down. If air resistance is small its downwards acceleration always equals *g* (around 9.81 m s⁻²).

Now look at the Worked Example. The answer is an approximation. Air resistance is significant over such distances. In the same way, air resistance affects the flight of a bullet fired into the air, so it does not come down at the same speed at which it left the gun.

Worked example

You hit a cricket ball vertically upwards at 40 m s⁻¹. How high does it go?

We have

$v = 0$ (at the top of the path)

$u = 40$ m s⁻¹ (call upwards positive, so *u* is positive)

$x = ?$

$a = -9.81$ m s⁻² (acceleration is downwards, so negative)

t (irrelevant)

so we use

$$v^2 = u^2 + 2ax$$

Numerically

$$0^2 = 40^2 + 2 \times (-9.81) \times x$$

$$0 = 1600 - 19.62\,x$$

$$x = 82 \text{ m}$$

Shooting horizontally and dropping

- Balance a short rule on a small fixed pivot and place two ball bearings as shown in Figure 5.3.
- Spin the rule quickly to drop one ball bearing vertically and knock the other one horizontally off the table at the same time.
- Compare the time at which they reach the ground.

Figure 5.3 *Shooting horizontally and dropping*

Horizontal projection

The above experiment shows that an object fired horizontally falls vertically with the same acceleration as one which is just dropped. A body that is thrown horizontally from the top of a cliff takes the same time to reach the bottom of the cliff as a body dropped vertically. The cartoon in Figure 5.4 shows this in another way.

Since air resistance is small, the horizontal velocity is constant, while the vertical velocity increases at a rate of 9.8 m s^{-2}. So for **projectile motion**, horizontal motion is independent of vertical motion, and the result is a curved path through the air called a parabola.

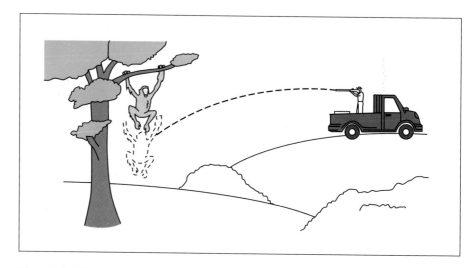

Figure 5.4 *The monkey let go at the same time as the hunter fired horizontally at it. It fell the same vertical distance as the bullet and, sadly, met its end!*

Measuring the speed of a snooker ball

- Use a cue to fire a snooker ball horizontally off the table and measure how far it goes, both horizontally and vertically (Figure 5.5).
- Calculate the time of flight from the vertical distance.
- From the time of flight and the horizontal distance travelled, calculate the horizontal velocity, assuming that it is constant.

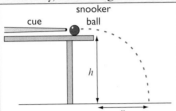

Figure 5.5 *Finding the speed of a horizontally projected snooker ball*

Worked example

A tennis ball passes horizontally just over the net and lands just inside the base line of the court. The net has a height of 1.07 m and is 11.9 m from the base line. Find the horizontal speed of the tennis ball. (Ignore air resistance and spin.)

Use vertical motion to find the time in the air. We have

$v = ?$ (not needed)

$u = 0$

$x = 1.07$ m

$a = 9.8$ m s^{-2}

$t = ?$

so we use

$x = ut + \frac{1}{2} at^2$

$\quad = \frac{1}{2} at^2$

$1.07 \text{ m} = \frac{1}{2} \times 9.8 \text{ m s}^{-2} \times t^2$

$\quad\quad = 4.9 \text{ m s}^{-2} \times t^2$

$t^2 = \dfrac{1.07 \text{ s}^2}{4.9}$

$\quad = 0.22 \text{ s}^2$

$t = 0.47$ s

Use horizontal motion to find speed (assumed constant):

$$\text{speed} = \frac{\text{distance}}{\text{time}} = \frac{11.9 \text{ m}}{0.47 \text{ s}} = 25.5 \text{ m s}^{-1} \text{ (or 57 mile/h)}$$

6 Newton's first law

Figure 6.1   Alone in space

Moving freely

Imagine a spacecraft in outer space (Figure 6.1), a long way away from other stars and planets, so that you could ignore the effect of any other bodies. You might say that the spacecraft is floating in space. It is not immersed in a fluid, but it behaves a bit as if it were. The spacecraft can move freely in all directions. It is not affected by other bodies. On Earth, you can imitate some aspects of the free movement of the body in space if you examine movement in one direction only, for instance the horizontal motion of something that can move freely horizontally.

Observing the motion of an air track glider

- Set up the air track so that it is horizontal and place a glider on it (Figure 6.2). Feel how freely the glider can move horizontally.
- Set the glider at rest and then leave it alone. Observe what happens.
- Next give the glider a push to set it moving. Again observe what happens.

Figure 6.2   A glider on an air track

What causes acceleration?

Within the imperfections of the apparatus, you find that a stationary glider on an air track remains stationary — its velocity remains at zero. And a moving glider keeps going at a constant velocity; it does not speed up or slow down. For both, the acceleration is zero.

If you want a freely moving body to accelerate, you need to push or pull it. When you do so, you are applying a **force** to it. Something has to cause a body to accelerate; that something is a force.

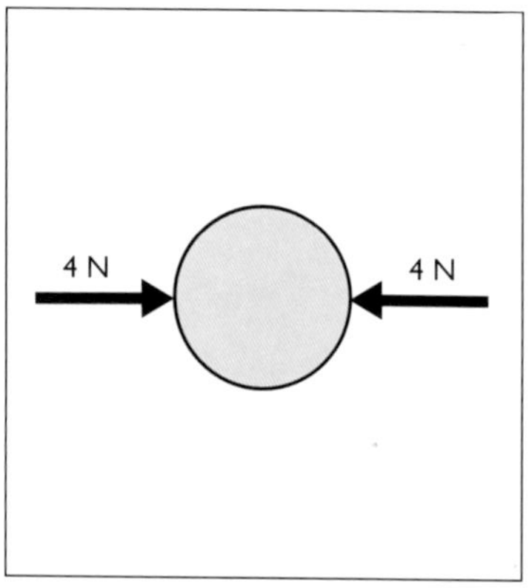

Newton's first law of motion

Forces are measured in newtons (N). If you apply a pair of equal and opposite forces to the glider, then it will not accelerate. The forces on the body cancel out. They are balanced, as in Figure 6.3.

Figure 6.3   Two balanced forces

If you apply more forces and the forces still balance, the body still will not accelerate, as in Figure 6.4.

When there are no forces acting on a body, or when the forces on a body cancel out, the body will not accelerate. The body is said to be in **equilibrium**.

What you need for acceleration is an unbalanced force or a set of forces that have a **resultant force** (or simply, resultant) in some direction, as in Figure 6.5.

Newton's first law of motion summarises these observations to one saying:

A body will remain at rest or continue to move with a constant velocity as long as the forces on it are balanced.

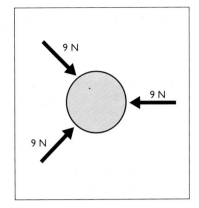

Figure 6.4   Three balanced forces

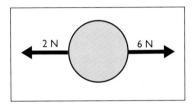

Figure 6.5   Two unbalanced forces: the resultant force is 4 N to the right

Inertia

A body behaves as though it is reluctant to change its velocity. In other words, a body will remain at rest or will continue to move with a constant velocity unless it is forced to do otherwise. This reluctance to change velocity is the **inertia** of the body.

It is much harder to change the velocity of a larger mass than a small one. The bigger the mass of a body, the larger its inertia.

Testing inertia

- Set up two tin cans as in Figure 6.6.
- Give each of the stationary tin cans a similar, sharp knock with the side of your hand. Observe the difference.
- Next pull back both cans to the same height and then release them. Try to stop each can as it reaches the bottom of its swing.

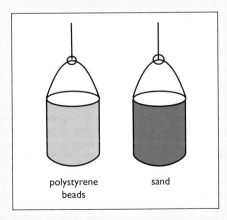

Figure 6.6   Testing inertia with suspended tin cans

23

Newton's second law

The relationship between force, mass and acceleration

- Set up the runway and tilt it just enough so that a trolley runs down it at constant speed when given a push.
- Use a forcemeter to apply a constant force to the trolley and measure the acceleration (Figure 7.1). Repeat for a range of forces and plot a graph of acceleration against force.
- Next repeat the experiment but this time use a constant force and add masses to the trolley.
- Measure the acceleration for a range of measured masses. Plot a graph of acceleration against 1/mass.

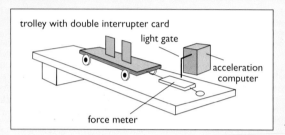

Figure 7.1   Accelerating a trolley

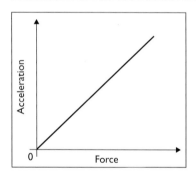

Figure 7.2   An acceleration–force graph for the trolley experiment

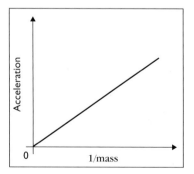

Figure 7.3   A graph of acceleration against 1/mass for the trolley

What determines the acceleration?

If the resultant force acting on a body increases, so does the acceleration; the acceleration of the body is directly proportional to the resultant force (Figure 7.2).

The same resultant force will give a smaller acceleration to a larger mass; acceleration is inversely proportional to mass (Figure 7.3).

These two results can be summarised by the equation

$$\text{force} \propto \text{mass} \times \text{acceleration}$$

or

$$\text{force} = k \times \text{mass} \times \text{acceleration} \quad \text{where } k \text{ is a constant}$$

In the International System, the value of the constant k is equal to 1, so the equation becomes

$$\text{force} = \text{mass} \times \text{acceleration}$$

The definition of the newton

The equation above also defines the newton, since

$$1\,\text{N} = 1\,\text{kg} \times 1\,\text{m s}^{-2}$$

So **one newton** is the resultant force that will give a mass of 1 kg an acceleration of 1 m s^{-2}. Some typical force values are listed in Table 7.1. An example of a force producing an acceleration is shown in Figure 7.4.

Table 7.1 *Typical force values*

1 N	the gravitational force on an apple
10 N	the gravitational force on 1 kg
100 N	a firm push
600 N	the gravitational force on you
10 000 N	the gravitational force on a car

Newton's second law of motion

It may seem obvious, but it is worth stating that the direction of acceleration is the same as the direction of the resultant force. If the resultant force is downwards, the acceleration is downwards. If the resultant force is west, so is the acceleration. This, combined with the above equation, produces one version of **Newton's second law of motion**, which states that:

The acceleration of a body is proportional to the resultant force and takes place in the direction of the force.

There is an alternative statement of Newton's second law in Chapter 16.

Newton's laws, like other scientific laws, attempt to describe or predict behaviour, as outlined in Table 7.2.

Figure 7.4 The Space Shuttle's booster rockets give a force of 24 000 000 N on a mass of 2 000 000 kg. What is the acceleration?

Table 7.2 *Laws*

Moral laws and laws of the land tell people what they should do
By contrast, physical laws, like Newton's laws, are just descriptions of the universe as we find it. They don't tell the universe how to behave

Worked example

A tractor pulls a tree-stump of mass 2000 kg along rough horizontal ground. The tractor exerts a horizontal force of 1300 N on the tree-stump, which accelerates at 50 mm s^{-2}. What is the frictional force between the tree-stump and the ground?

Resultant force $F = ma$ so

$F = 2000 \text{ kg} \times 50 \times 10^{-3} \text{ m s}^{-2} = 100 \text{ N}$

Since resultant force = pull of tractor − friction

100 N = 1300 N − friction

friction = 1200 N

Newton's third law

Figure 8.1   *A spacecraft alone in outer space*

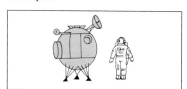

Figure 8.2   *You and the spacecraft exert no force on each other, so both are in equilibrium*

Figure 8.3   *What happens when you push the spacecraft?*

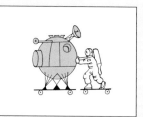

Figure 8.4   *What happens when you push now you are on wheels?*

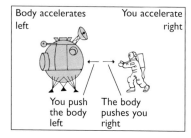

Figure 8.5   *The body accelerates to the left; you accelerate to the right*

A body with no forces

Think again about a spacecraft in outer space, a long way from other bodies, so you could imagine that there were no forces acting on the spacecraft (Figure 8.1).

You know from Newton's first law that, if the spacecraft were stationary, it would stay stationary. If it were moving in a straight line, it would keep on moving at the same velocity. Now imagine that you were in space too, just beside the spacecraft and stationary relative to it. Since there are no forces on you or the spacecraft, you stay stationary relative to it (Figure 8.2).

A single force?

Now think what happens when you apply a single force to the spacecraft by pushing it (Figure 8.3).

Both you and the spacecraft are a long way from other bodies. So you would be standing on nothing. You can think about what would happen if it did occur. This is called 'doing a thought experiment'. An experiment in the laboratory helps to understand what might happen.

Pushing the body

- Find a large body that is on very smooth wheels.
- Stand on free-moving rollers, or a good skateboard yourself to imitate something of the free movement of deep space.
- Observe what happens when you push the body (Figure 8.4).

Pairs of forces

When you push something to the left, it accelerates to the left. But that isn't the end of the story; you also accelerate, but to the right. It helps to draw separate diagrams of both you and whatever you are pushing to show what is happening to each (Figure 8.5).

You started off thinking about a single force and a very simple situation in which that force might occur. But when you apply a single force to anything, that body applies another force to you.

Forces only occur in pairs

The body accelerates to the left because you push it to the left. And you accelerate to the right because it pushes you to the right.

The fact is that you can't have one force on its own. When any one body exerts a force on a second body, the second body exerts a force on the first body. One force cannot occur without the other.

Who is pushing whom?

- Stand with a friend, each of you on a skateboard, and pull a rope connecting you. Observe what happens.
- Then hold the rope and get your friend to do the pulling. Observe again.
- Then both pull.
- Repeat the experiments using spring forcemeters to measure the forces you each exert (Figure 8.6). Record the measurements.

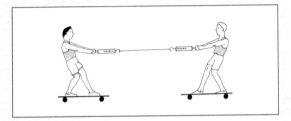

Figure 8.6   Measuring the force you exert

Newton's third law of motion

Look at Figure 8.7. When you burn the string holding the two spring-loaded trolleys together, they accelerate apart. If you measure their masses and their accelerations, you find that the forces that they exert on each other are equal. It doesn't matter which trolley has the spring, or whether both do. While trolley A pushes B, trolley B pushes A with an equal force in the opposite direction.

The important principle behind these observations led Newton to formulate his third law. As you would expect by now, a single force on its own cannot exist. There are always two forces and **Newton's third law of motion** says about these forces:

> While body A exerts a force on body B, body B exerts an equal and opposite force on body A.

Perhaps the most important and difficult point to appreciate about this pair of forces is that they act on different bodies. The third-law pair of forces between bodies A and B consists of a single force on body A, and a single equal and opposite force on body B. Each of these forces has its separate effect on a separate body. The two forces do not cancel each other.

There is more about these two forces in the next two chapters with a complete statement of Newton's third law in Chapter 10.

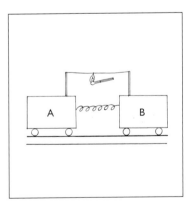

Figure 8.7   When you burn the string, the two trolleys spring apart

9 Types of forces

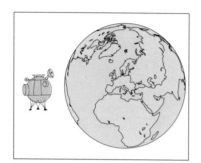

Figure 9.1   *There is a gravitational force between the spacecraft and the Earth*

Earth pulls spacecraft

Figure 9.2   *The Earth pulls the spacecraft right, so the spacecraft accelerates to the right*

Acting at a distance

The forces that bodies in space are most likely to experience are gravitational. Imagine a spacecraft near to a planet, as in Figure 9.1. The planet pulls the spacecraft towards the planet (Figure 9.2). And, just as you would expect, the spacecraft pulls the planet with an equal force towards the spacecraft (Figure 9.3).

The force on the spacecraft is equal and opposite to the force on the planet, and the forces have the same line of action and act for the same time.

The two bodies are exerting a force on each other without being in contact. These are gravitational forces; they act at a distance. Gravitational forces occur between all bodies of all sizes and attract them together. Gravitational forces are one of the four different types of force that exist.

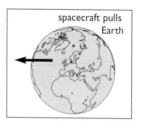

spacecraft pulls Earth

Figure 9.3   *The spacecraft pulls the Earth left, so the Earth accelerates to the left*

Gravity and gravitational fields

Masses around any body experience gravitational forces. The region in which they experience this force is the body's gravitational field. The gravitational force that a planet applies to a body is called its **weight**. When you are standing on the Earth, the Earth pulls you towards it and provides your weight. You pull the Earth with an equal and opposite force.

Investigating electrostatic forces

- Rub a polythene rod with a duster and then suspend it from a thread.
- Rub another rod and suspend it too.
- Bring them together (Figure 9.4) and observe what happens.
- Draw diagrams to show the forces on each rod.
- Repeat with two acetate rods, then with one polythene and one acetate rod.

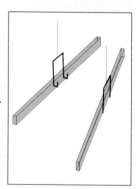

Figure 9.4   *Investigating electrostatic forces*

Electrostatic forces

When you rub a polythene rod with a duster, the rod becomes charged negatively. Two negatively charged rods repel, as do two positively charged rods; but a positive and a negative charge attract (Figure 9.5). These forces are electrostatic forces. Like gravitational forces, electrostatic forces act at a distance.

Investigating magnetic forces

- Bring the north-seeking ends of two magnets together.
- Observe what happens and then draw diagrams to show the forces on each end.
- Repeat with two south-seeking ends and then with one north-seeking and one south-seeking.

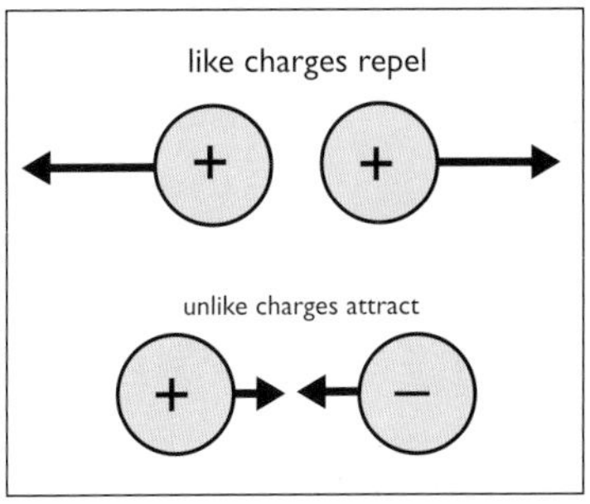

Electromagnetic forces

Between two magnets, or between a magnet and another piece of magnetic material, there are magnetic forces. These forces, too, act at a distance. The forces between static charges and between magnets are related. One of Einstein's (Figure 9.6) great pieces of work was to suggest that electrostatic forces and magnetic forces are just the same type of force viewed from relatively different positions. His theory of special relativity made it possible to understand them as a single force, called the electromagnetic force.

Figure 9.5 Electrostatic forces between charges

Nuclear forces

There are forces that act inside the nucleus of an atom which are neither gravitational nor electromagnetic. These nuclear forces are important—they hold the nucleus together. Electrostatic repulsion alone would cause the positively charged protons in the nucleus to fly apart. But there is a force, the strong nuclear force, which binds them together.

The weak nuclear force is involved, for example, in beta decay when a neutron decays to a proton, with the emission of an electron. The nuclear forces act over very small distances and are often referred to as short-range forces.

Forces are often described as interactions, particularly when small particles are involved. This helps to emphasise that they always involve the effect of one body acting on another.

Contact forces

When you push a car, pick up a book or push a cork into a bottle, the forces are not obviously gravitational, electromagnetic or nuclear. These are called **contact forces**, because the bodies between which they exist are very close together. Contact forces are, in fact, electrostatic forces acting over very short distances. They are caused by forces between the outer layers of electrons of the two bodies in contact. When you push something, the electrons on the outside of your hand repel the electrons on the outside of the body you are pushing. Frictional forces, forces on bodies moving through liquids, and air resistance are all contact forces.

Figure 9.6 Einstein's success in providing a unified theory of electricity and magnetism encouraged him and others in the search for a theory, a unified field theory, that would describe all the different types of force.

Free-body force diagrams

Figure 10.1   Situation diagram for a man near the Earth

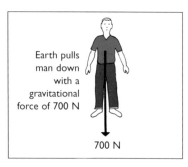

Figure 10.2   Free-body force diagram for a man near the Earth

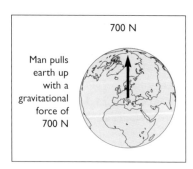

Figure 10.3   Free-body force diagram for the Earth near a man

Situation diagrams and free-body force diagrams

You know that forces always occur in pairs, one force acting on one body, and one force on another body. If you draw both these forces in the same diagram it is confusing because, in all but the simplest situations, it is unclear which forces act on which body. Free-body force diagrams are a neat and effective way of showing the forces on a body; they are diagrams of a *single* body, showing the forces on that body *only*.

Figure 10.1 shows a situation diagram for a man near the Earth. Figures 10.2 and 10.3 show two *free-body force diagrams*, one for the man and one for the Earth. Each free-body force diagram shows a single body, and the forces on that body alone. Free-body force diagrams may look like situation diagrams, but there is one really important difference. In the man's free-body force diagram, he is on his own, without the Earth. That does not mean that the Earth doesn't exist, just that the diagram is only about what is happening to the man.

If you need to draw a free-body force diagram, it sometimes helps first to sketch a rough situation diagram with all the bodies, and then to draw a separate free-body force diagram for each body.

Describing forces

The labels on the forces in the free-body force diagrams for the man and the planet describe the forces fully. These descriptions consist of five parts:

The <u>Earth</u> pulls the <u>man</u> <u>down</u> with a <u>gravitational</u> force of <u>700 N</u>

The description states
- what is exerting the force
- on what the force is exerted
- the direction of the force
- the type of the force
- the size of the force.

Similarly,

The <u>man</u> pulls the <u>Earth</u> <u>up</u> with a <u>gravitational</u> force of <u>700 N</u>

Descriptions like this help identify Newton III pairs of forces.

Identifying Newton III pairs of forces

From this work on free-body force diagrams, you should be able to see that the forces in a Newton III pair of forces have the same line of action – if you extend the force lines on the diagram of the situation, then they will pass through each other. The forces also act for the same time. In addition, you should realise that the two forces of a Newton III pair have to be the same type of force. If A pulls on B with a gravitational force, then B pulls on A with a gravitational force also. This information allows a complete statement of **Newton's third law**:

> While a body A exerts a force on a body B, body B exerts a force on body A. The forces are equal, opposite and of the same type; they have the same line of action and act for the same time.

If you have described one force fully, then you can identify the Newton III pair to this force from its description. Simply exchange the two bodies in the statement and reverse the direction of the force. For example:

The <u>planet</u> pulls the <u>man</u> <u>down</u> with a <u>gravitational</u> force of <u>700 N</u>

The <u>man</u> pulls the <u>planet</u> <u>up</u> with a <u>gravitational</u> force of <u>700 N</u>

So if

<u>Freda</u> pushes <u>Jo</u> <u>left</u> with a <u>contact</u> force of <u>35 N</u>

<u>Jo</u> pushes <u>Freda</u> <u>right</u> with a <u>contact</u> force of <u>35 N</u>

Figure 10.4   Situation diagram for a man standing on the Earth

Standing on a planet

Two bodies often exert more than one pair of forces on each other. Think about a body resting on the surface of a planet. Figure 10.4 shows the diagram of this situation for a man on the Earth, and Figures 10.5 and 10.6 show the two free-body force diagrams for the man and the Earth.

As before, there is a pair of gravitational forces between the man and the Earth, one on the man and one on the Earth. But there are also contact forces, again one on the man and one on the Earth.

First think about the forces on the man. The Earth pulls the man down with a gravitational force. The Earth also pushes the man up with a contact force.

Now think about the forces on the Earth. The man pulls the Earth up with a gravitational force, and also pushes the Earth down with a contact force.

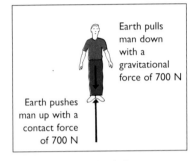

Figure 10.5   Free-body force diagram for a man standing on the Earth. The man is in equilibrium because the two forces on him are equal and opposite

Differences between Newton I and Newton III

Figure 10.5 shows the free-body force diagram for a man standing on the Earth. The man is in equilibrium. From this you can deduce that the forces on the man are balanced: the upward force on him is equal to the downward force. But these forces are *not* a Newton III pair. There are a number of reasons why we know that.

First, the upward force from the Earth and the downward force from the Earth both act on the same body, the man. With a Newton III pair, the forces act on different bodies.

Secondly, the upward force on the man is a contact force and the downward force is gravitational. With a Newton III pair, the forces are of the same type.

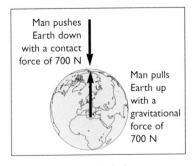

Figure 10.6   Free-body force diagram for the Earth. The Earth is in equilibrium because the two forces on it are equal and opposite

Thirdly, these two forces are only equal when the man is in equilibrium, and he need not necessarily be so. As you know, if the man is above the Earth as in Figure 10.1, there is no contact force but there is still a gravitational force. With a Newton III pair the forces are *always* equal and opposite, and one force cannot occur without the other.

The man in Figure 10.5 just happens to be in equilibrium under the action of two forces and so, in accordance with Newton I, these forces are equal and opposite.

These differences are summarised in Table 10.1. You might like to think about how they apply to some of the forces on the bodies in Figure 10.7.

Table 10.1 *Some important differences between Newton I and Newton III*

Newton I	Newton III
A law about the forces *on a single body*	A law about a pair of forces *on two different bodies*
Concerns *any number of forces*	Always concerns *two forces only*
The forces can be *different types*	Always the *same type* of force
If two forces *and* body in equilibrium, forces are equal and opposite	Forces *always* equal and opposite
Only applies when a body is in equilibrium	*Always* applies

Figure 10.7   Astronauts working in space

Adding and splitting up forces

Adding forces

Forces are vector quantities. Like displacement, velocity and acceleration, they have both size and direction, but, unlike other vectors, they also have lines of action. Like other vector quantities, if you wish to add forces together to find their resultant, you need to take account of their directions.

Here are some examples. In Figure 11.1, Freda and Jo are pulling in opposite directions with forces of 600 N and 700 N. As the force diagram shows, it is easy to see that the resultant is 100 N in the direction that Jo is pulling. If they push in the same direction (Figure 11.2), the resultant is 1300 N. When Freda and Jo push at right angles (Figure 11.3), you need to use a vector diagram to find the resultant force, as follows.

Drawing vector force diagrams

Represent the vectors you wish to add, in size and direction, with lines on a vector diagram. Draw the lines one after another, starting each line where the one before ends (Figure 11.4). The resultant is the line from where you start to where you end.

You can work out the resultant either by drawing the vectors to scale, or by using trigonometry. If you use trigonometry, draw a diagram roughly to scale first, so that you can check if the resultant is roughly correct.

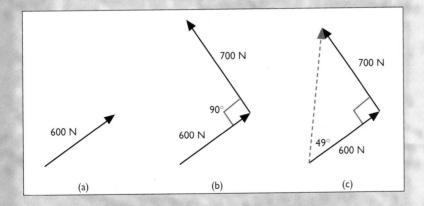

Figure 11.4   Drawing the resultant for Figure 11.3: (a) first draw one of the vectors; (b) then draw the other, at 90°, from the end of the first one; (c) the resultant is the line that completes the triangle

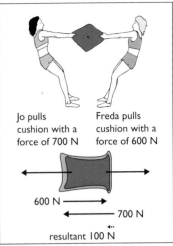

Figure 11.1   Freda and Jo are pulling a cushion. What is the resultant force on it if Jo pulls with a force of 700 N and Freda with 600 N?

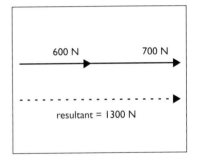

Figure 11.2   What is the resultant force of Freda and Jo pushing in the same direction on a rock?

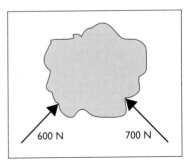

Figure 11.3   What is the resultant now Freda and Jo push the rock at right angles?

Three-force equilibrium

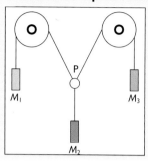

- Set up the pulleys and mass hangers as shown in Figure 11.5.
- Hang masses on the three mass hangers and let them move until stable. Draw the string pattern on the paper behind the pulleys.
- Determine the forces on point P by measuring the masses.
- Draw a vector diagram to find the resultant of the two upward forces. Check that this is equal and opposite to the downward force.

Figure 11.5   Three forces in equilibrium

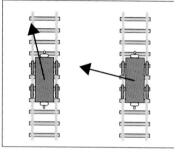

Figure 11.6   The more you pull directly along the track, the more effective you are

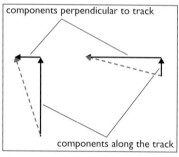

Figure 11.7   Your pull on the truck can be split into two components

Resolving forces

In the same way that you can combine forces to make a single resultant, you can think of a single force as made up of two or more parts, called **components**. It is often useful to split a vector up like this and think of the two parts separately.

Imagine pulling a railway truck along a track (Figure 11.6). You will obviously be much more effective the more directly you pull along the track. You can use components to calculate how effective.

In this situation, it is useful to think of the single applied force as being made up of two components, one along the track in the direction in which the truck will move, and the other perpendicular to the track.

Figure 11.7 shows two force diagrams, with components along the track and perpendicular to the track, having resultants that are the same as the single forces on the diagrams in Figure 11.6. The components along the track are useful in pulling the truck forward. The components perpendicular to the track are not. The more directly forward you pull, the bigger the forward component.

Vertical and horizontal components

- Hang the spring balance as shown in Figure 11.8. Measure the vertical force needed to support mass m_1 and check that it agrees with the weight of the mass.
- Pull the mass m_1 to the right with a string over the pulley attached to mass m_2 (Figure 11.9) and calculate the horizontal force that is pulling mass m_1 aside. Measure the new force on the spring balance and the angle between this balance and the vertical.
- Repeat for a range of masses m_2 and show your results in a table.
- Try to find a mathematical connection between the forces you measure and the angle.

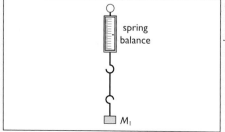

Figure 11.8 What vertical force is needed to support the mass?

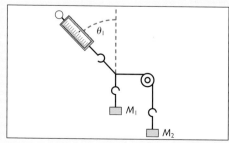

Figure 11.9 What is the force on the spring balance now? What is the angle?

Calculating components

Figure 11.10 shows the free-body force diagram for the knot in the string in Figure 11.9. The force F_{m_1} from mass m_1 pulls the knot down, and the force F_{m_2} from mass m_2 pulls the knot to the right. Since the knot is in equilibrium, you know that the force F from the spring balance must balance these two forces. The vertical component F_v of F must be equal to F_{m_1} and the horizontal component F_h of F must be equal to F_{m_2} (As Figure 11.11a shows).

From Figure 11.11b you can see that $\cos \theta_1 = F_v/F$; so $F_v = F \cos \theta_1$. Similarly $\cos \theta_2 = F_h/F$; so $F_h = F \cos \theta_2$.

This relationship enables you to find the magnitude of any component of any force in any direction. The component is the original force multiplied by the cosine of the angle between the force and the direction of the component you are interested in.

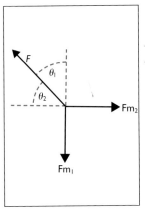

Figure 11.10 Free-body force diagram for the knot in Figure 11.9

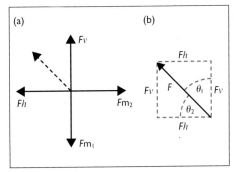

Figure 11.11 Horizontal and vertical components of the force in Figure 11.10

As with vector addition, you can use either scale diagrams or trigonometry to find components. But even when using trigonometry, make your diagrams roughly to scale, to give a guide to the approximate size of your answers. An example is shown in Figure 11.12.

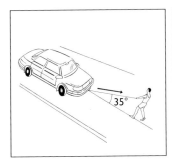

Figure 11.12a Bill pulls a car along with a force of 400 N at an angle of 35° to the direction of motion

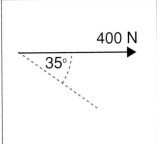

Figure 11.12b First draw a line to represent the vector in size and direction, Then draw a line in the direction in which you are interested through the starting point of the vector

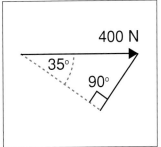

Figure 11.12c Draw a perpendicular to the line from the other end of the vector

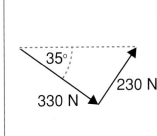

Figure 11.12d The triangle you have drawn gives the components in the two perpendicular directions. In this case, Bill's force is equivalent to 330 N in the forward direction and 230 N perpendicular to that direction

Harder free-body force diagrams

More than two bodies

If you draw free-body force diagrams for all the bodies in a complicated situation, it can help you to understand how the forces on the bodies relate to each other.

The cat, the table and the planet

Figure 12.1 shows a cat sitting on a table. Assume that the cat, the table and the planet are in equilibrium, First draw the three bodies separately (Figure 12.2) to start a free-body force diagram for each.

Figure 12.1   The cat, the table and the planet

Figure 12.2   The cat, table and planet separately

Forces on the cat

Look carefully at Figure 12.3. The third word in both of the force descriptions is 'cat'. The planet pulls the cat down, and the table pushes the cat up. Grammatically, the object of both of these sentences is the cat. This is because both of these forces are acting on the cat. (If you describe forces simply like this, it helps you to check that you have included only forces that act on that body on a body's diagram.) These two forces are the only significant forces on the cat, and, since the cat is in equilibrium, the forces must be equal and opposite, in agreement with Newton I.

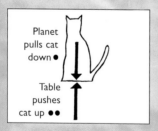

Figure 12.3   Free-body force diagram for the cat

Forces on the table

There are two downward forces on the table (Figure 12.4): the planet pulls it down, and the cat pushes it down. The planet itself pushes the table up. Now the third word in each force description is 'table'. The table is in equilibrium, so, as a consequence of Newton I, the upwards force must be equal to the sum of the downwards forces.

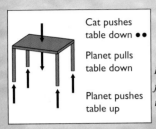

Cat pushes
table down ●●

Planet pulls
table down

Planet pushes
table up

Figure 12.4 Free-body force diagram for the table

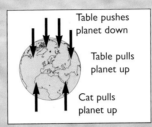

Table pushes
planet down

Table pulls
planet up

Cat pulls
planet up

Figure 12.5 Free-body force diagram for the planet

Forces on the planet

In Figure 12.5, you can see the forces on the planet. Both the table and the cat pull the planet up, and the table pushes the planet down. The planet is in equilibrium, so the sum of the forces upwards must be equal to the downwards force.

There are, of course, gravitational forces between the cat and the table, but these are so small that you can ignore them. The single and double bullets show two Newton III force pairs. Work out the others.

Perpendicular and tangential contact forces

The contact forces between the cat, the table and the planet in Figures 12.3 to 12.5 act perpendicularly to surfaces that are in contact. But surfaces like this can also produce forces tangential to the surface (along the surface). These **tangential forces** are due to friction.

The cat, the sloping table and the planet

This situation is summarised in Figures 12.6 to 12.8. The cat remains in equilibrium because the table provides an upwards force on the cat that is equal to the gravitational force on the cat. You can think of the single upwards force on the cat as being made up of two components: a perpendicular contact force and a tangential contact force of friction. These two components together are equal and opposite to the downwards gravitational force.

Figure 12.6 The cat, the sloping table and the planet

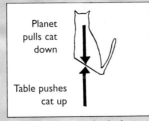

Planet
pulls cat
down

Table pushes
cat up

Figure 12.7 Free-body force diagram for the cat

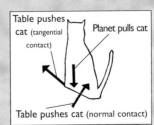

Table pushes
cat (tangential
contact)

Planet pulls cat

Table pushes cat (normal contact)

Figure 12.8 Components of upwards force on the cat

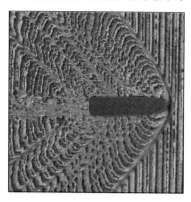

Figure 12.9   Here, you can see the disturbance of the air, which is the source of the viscous drag on the bullet

Frictional forces

You get frictional forces when one surface might slide over another; friction opposes the relative motion. Frictional forces also arise when bodies move through fluids—gases or liquids. As the body moves, it has to push the fluid out of the way, and this results in a force, called **drag**, that opposes the relative motion. The forces partly arise from the need to accelerate the mass of the fluid out of the way of the object, and partly because of viscous friction, due to intermolecular forces between the surface of the moving object and the fluid. Figure 12.9 shows an example.

Bodies moving at constant velocity

You know that, when a body is moving with constant velocity, it is in equilibrium. The forces on it are balanced. Figures 12.10 to 12.17 show free-body force diagrams for various bodies which are in equilibrum:

• *Aircraft in level flight:*   The air surrounding an aircraft produces three contact forces on it (Figure 12.10). The aircraft's jets push air backwards, and the Newton III pair to this is the force of the air pushing the aircraft forwards. This is the thrust. As air travels over the upper and lower surfaces of the wing, it produces an upwards force called lift. The air produces drag as the aircraft travels through it. If the aircraft is travelling at constant velocity, the forces on it are balanced. Then, the drag is equal to the thrust, and the lift is equal to the weight.

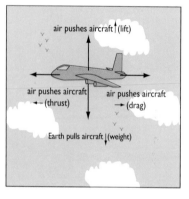

Figure 12.10   Aircraft in level flight

• *Aircraft climbing:*   If an aircraft is travelling at constant velocity, the forces on it are balanced, whether the aircraft is climbing (Figure 12.11) or in level flight. The upwards components of the thrust and lift are equal to the weight plus the downward component of the drag. The forward component of the thrust and the lift is equal to the backward component of the weight and the drag.

• *Horse pulling cart:*   The horse pulls the cart at a steady speed along the surface of the planet (Figure 12.12). We first think about the forces on the horse (Figure 12.13). The horse pushes the planet backwards, so the planet pushes the horse forwards. The force of the planet down is equal to the force of the planet surface upwards; and the force of the planet to the left is equal to the force of the cart to the right.

Now consider the cart (Figure 12.14). The cart is in equilibrium, so the force of the planet down is equal to the force of the planet surface upwards; and the force of the horse to the left is equal to the force of the ground to the right.

For the planet, too (Figure 12.15), the sum of the forces in any direction is zero.

• *Four-wheel-drive car:*   All the car's wheels push the ground backwards (Figure 12.16). The Newton III pairs to these forces are the forces of the ground pushing the car forwards. These frictional contact forces are the driving forces of the car.

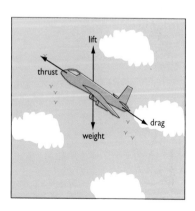

Figure 12.11   Aircraft climbing

• *Front-wheel-drive car:* In this case (Figure 12.17), only the front wheels push the ground backwards, so the ground pushes these two wheels forwards. The rear wheels are not driven; the ground pushes them backwards.

Figure 12.12   Horse pulling cart

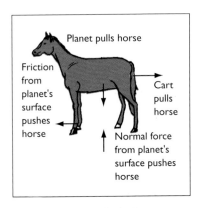

Figure 12.13   Free-body force diagram for the horse

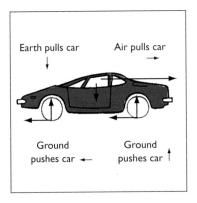

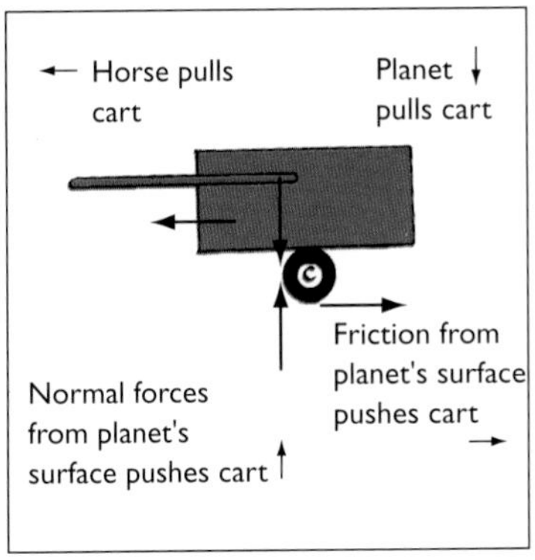

Figure 12.14   Free-body force diagram for the cart

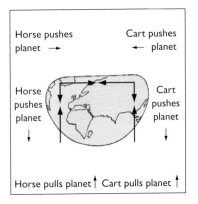

Figure 12.15   Free-body force diagram for the planet

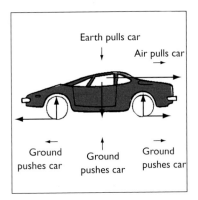

Figure 12.16   Four-wheel-drive car

Figure 12.17   Front-wheel-drive car

Moments and couples

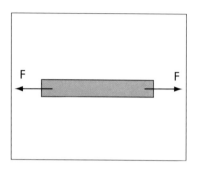

Figure 13.1   This rod is under tension

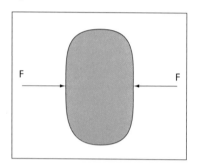

Figure 13.2   This ball is under compression

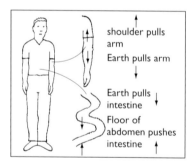

Figure 13.3   Gravity and supporting forces put some parts of your body into tension and some into compression

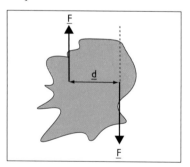

Figure 13.4   This pair of forces is a couple, which causes rotation

Two forces

Very often a body has a pair of equal and opposite forces acting on it. If the weight of the rod in Figure 13.1 is so little that you can ignore it, the rod will be in equilibrium if the leftward force is equal to the rightward force. Even though the rod is in equilibrium, it is still in a state of **tension** caused by forces that stretch it. The ball in Figure 13.2 is also in equilibrium. But it is in **compression** caused by the pair of forces that squash it. Parts of your body are in compression and other parts are in tension (Figure 13.3).

Turning moments

If a pair of equal and opposite forces, which are not in line, act on a body, they tend to cause the body to rotate (Figure 13.4). The forces cause no linear acceleration, because they provide equal and opposite linear effects. But they have a rotational effect. They provide a **couple**. The body on which they act will be in *translational* equilibrium, but not in *rotational* equilibrium.

The ability of the couple to cause rotation depends on the size of the forces and how far they are apart. The size of this effect is called the turning moment or just the moment.

You can find the **moment of a couple** by multiplying one of the forces F by the perpendicular distance d between them. In Figure 13.4, the moment = Fd. Moments of different sizes are shown in Figure 13.5.

Turning moment is calculated by multiplying a force by a distance which is perpendicular to the line of action of the force. Moment is measured in newton metres (N m). The physical quantity of work is also calculated by multiplying a force by a distance, but in this case the force is multiplied by a distance in the direction of the force and also has units of newton metres (see Chapter 17). By convention, the unit of work is called a joule and the unit of moment is always referred to as a newton metre.

The moment of a force

You can calculate the moment of a single force about any point. The **moment of a force** is the product of the force and the perpendicular distance from the point that you are measuring (Figure 13.6).

Torque

Often more than two forces cause a turning moment; for instance, more than four different forces, at different times, cause the turning moment on the crankshaft of a car. A **torque** is the turning moment caused by a system of two or more forces that tend to cause rotation.

Neither a couple nor a torque has any resultant force in any direction, so neither causes any linear acceleration. They have no translational effect.

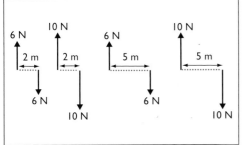

Figure 13.5 The largest moments occur with large forces and a large perpendicular distance

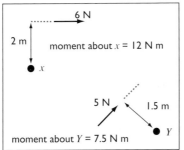

Figure 13.6 The moment of a force about a point

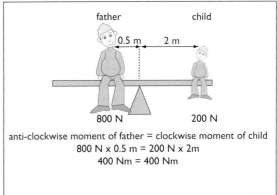

anti-clockwise moment of father = clockwise moment of child
800 N x 0.5 m = 200 N x 2m
400 Nm = 400 Nm

Figure 13.7 The father's anticlockwise moment equals the child's clockwise moment

Principle of moments

If a body is in equilibrium, you know that the sum of the forces in any direction must be zero. There is another condition for equilibrium. If a body is in equilibrium, the sum of the moments turning the body one way must equal the sum of the moments turning it in the opposite direction. The sum of the moments about any point must be zero. This is the **principle of moments**. The moments for a father and child balanced on a see-saw are shown in Figure 13.7.

Forces on bridge supports

- A lorry on a bridge can be modelled using apparatus set up as in Figure 13.8. We shall use the model bridge to investigate how the forces on the two supports change as a lorry moves over a bridge.
- Set up the apparatus as shown. Measure the forces on the two supports as the lorry moves over the bridge.
- For each position of the lorry, calculate the moment of the forces about each support (Figure 13.9), the sum of the upward forces and the sum of the downward forces.

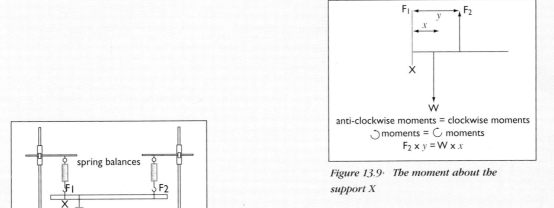

anti-clockwise moments = clockwise moments
↺ moments = ↻ moments
$F_2 \times y = W \times x$

Figure 13.9 The moment about the support X

Figure 13.8 A model for a lorry on a bridge

Finding the centre of gravity of a body

- Hang the body from a suitable point. Draw a vertical line through the point of support when the body is balanced (Figure 13.10).
- Repeat with another balancing point. Where the two lines intersect is the centre of gravity (Figure 13.11).
- Repeat again with a third line to check.

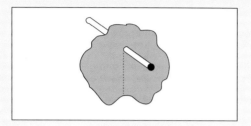

Figure 13.10   A body hanging from a point

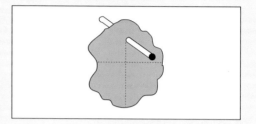

Figure 13.11   The body hanging from a new point

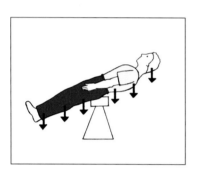

Figure 13.12   Gravity acts on all parts of a body

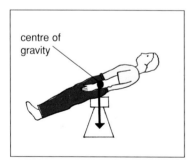

Figure 13.13   You can consider that all the weight acts through the centre of gravity

Centre of gravity

When a body is in a gravitational field, each part of the body has a gravitational force on it (Figure 13.12). If you support a body, each of these gravitational forces has a moment about the point of support.

With the support in the right place, the body is balanced. The sum of all the moments of the different parts of the body is then zero about the point of support. This occurs when the support is vertically in line with the body's **centre of gravity**, the point at which all the weight appears to act. For balancing and for linear motion you can consider that a body's whole weight acts through the centre of gravity (Figure 13.13).

For spherically symmetrical bodies, the centre of gravity is always in the centre. For other rigid bodies, you can consider the centre of gravity to be fixed, even though it depends a little on the orientation of the body.

If a body changes its shape, the centre of gravity will change position. If you bend forwards at your waist, your centre of gravity will be somewhere outside your body.

Sometimes you will encounter the term **centre of mass**. This is the place at which all the mass appears to be. For gravitational purposes, the centre of mass is in the same position as the centre of gravity, and you can treat the two terms as if they were the same.

Finding the mass of a retort stand

- Balance a retort stand on its own to find its centre of gravity (Figure 13.14).
- Then, with the help of a set of masses, balance it about a different point (Figure 13.15).
- Calculate the clockwise moments of the set of masses. This is equal to the anticlockwise moment of the mass of the retort stand.
- From this, calculate the mass of the retort stand.

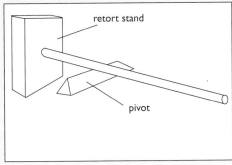

Figure 13.14   Find the centre of gravity by balancing the retort stand alone

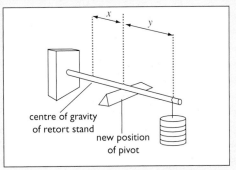

Figure 13.15   Then balance the retort stand with a known mass on the end

Measuring an unknown mass

- Set up the apparatus as in Figure 13.16.
- For a range of positions of the unknown mass M, find where you should put the known mass m to balance it.
- Anticlockwise moments = clockwise moments

$$Mgx = mgy$$
$$y = (M/m)x$$

- Plot a graph of y against x. Measure the slope, which is M/m, and then find M.

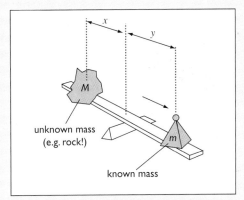

Figure 13.16   You can use the principle of moments to measure an unknown mass

14 Solving statics problems

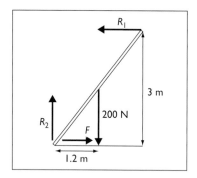

Figure 14.1   Free-body force diagram for a ladder resting against a wall

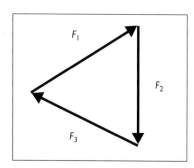

Figure 14.2   If three forces have no resultant, they must form a complete vector triangle

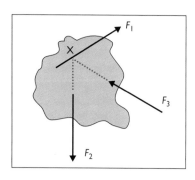

Figure 14.3   All the forces cross at X, so there is no moment

Conditions for equilibrium

Statics is the study of forces in systems that are stationary, whereas *dynamics* is the study of forces in systems that are moving. In A-level physics, the only statics situations that you need to know about are those in which the forces are *coplanar*, which means that all the forces are confined to a single plane.

When a body is in equilibrium, the sum of the forces in any direction is zero and the sum of the moments about any axis is zero. These conditions mean that you can usually write down three equations:

- equation (1) states that forces in any one direction are zero
- equation (2) states that forces in any other direction are zero
- equation (3) states that the moments about any point are zero

You can choose the directions and the point to make things easy: the two directions are usually horizontal and vertical. It is often helpful to choose a point through which at least two forces pass to simplify the moments equation.

For example, Figure 14.1 shows a free-body force diagram for a ladder resting against a wall. In this case your three equations could be:

- equation (1): the resultant vertical force must be zero
- equation (2): the resultant horizontal force must be zero
- equation (3): the anticlockwise moment of R_1 about the point of contact with the floor must equal the clockwise moment of the weight about the same point

So the equations would be:

$$R_2 - 200 \text{ N} = 0 \qquad (1)$$

$$R_1 - F = 0 \qquad (2)$$

$$R_1 \times 3 \text{ m} = 200 \text{ N} \times 1.2 \text{ m} \qquad (3)$$

From equation (1), you can calculate that $R_2 = 200$ N.

From equation (3), you can calculate that $R_1 = 80$ N.

So from equation (2), you can calculate that $F = 80$ N.

Special rules for situations involving three forces

When a body is in equilibrium under the action of three forces that are not parallel, two useful rules apply.

The first is that when you draw the forces head-to-tail one after another, they must form a closed triangle (Figure 14.2). Drawing them head-to-tail is the same as adding them with a vector diagram. If a number of forces have no resultant, when you draw them head-to-tail, the end of the last one must be at the start of the first.

The second condition is that all three forces must pass through a single point (Figure 14.3). If they don't pass through the same point, the body is *not* in equilibrium, (Figure 14.4).

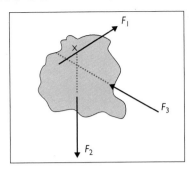

Figure 14.4   The two forces F_1 and F_2 cross at X, but F_3 does not. So F_3 has a moment about X and the body is not in equilibrium

Struts and ties

- Struts and ties are both parts of structures that help in supporting them. Struts are rigid components which are in compression. Ties are in tension and may therefore be flexible components like strings or wires.

- Test the arrangements shown in Figure 14.5. The spring balance, weight and bench provide three forces on the rule.

- Sketch a free-body force diagram for the rule in each situation and show that all the forces pass through a single point.

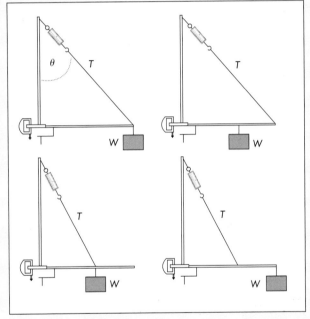

Figure 14.5   Arrangements of struts and ties

Answering statics problems

There are many situations in which you need to find two or three unknown forces on a body in equilibrium, on which one known force is acting.

1   Look for the simplest of the unknown forces.
2   Take moments about a point through which the other one or two unknown forces pass.
3a EITHER: resolve horizontally and vertically to find the other unknown(s).
3b OR: take moments about another point to calculate the other unknown(s).

Worked example

Figure 14.6 shows a trapdoor of weight 240 N held up by a horizontal tie. Calculate the tension in the tie and the horizontal and vertical components of the force at the hinge.

First draw a free-body force diagram for the trapdoor, as in Figure 14.7. The force at the hinge is represented by its vertical component F_v and horizontal component F_H. The only vertical forces are F_v and the weight of the trap. So F_v must be 240 N.

The simplest way to find T is to take moments about the hinge. Both F_v and F_H act through the hinge, and therefore have no moment about it. So

$$\text{anticlockwise moments} = \text{clockwise moments}$$

$$T \times 3\text{ m} = 240\text{ N} \times 2\text{ m}$$

$$T = \frac{480}{3}\text{ N}$$

$$= 160\text{ N}$$

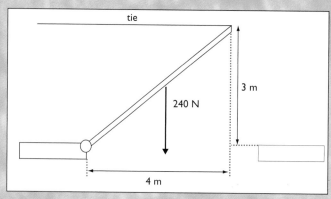

Figure 14.6   Trapdoor

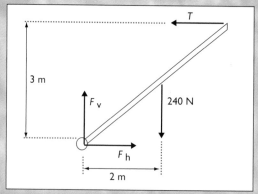

Figure 14.7   Free-body force diagram for the trapdoor

Conservation of momentum

A colliding pellet

- Fire the air-rifle pellet through two foil switches (Figure 15.1) and use a fast timer to measure the time between the two foils breaking.
- Measure the distance between the switches and calculate the speed of the pellet.
- Now measure the masses of a pellet and of an air track glider carrying some Plasticine (Figure 15.2).
- Place the glider at rest on the air track and fire a pellet so that it embeds in the Plasticine. Use the light gate to find the velocity of the glider after the collision.
- Try to find a connection between velocity and masses for the pellet and the glider.

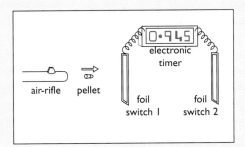

Figure 15.1   Direct timing of a pellet's flight

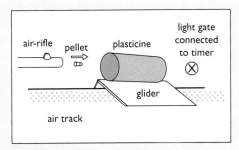

Figure 15.2   What is the velocity of the glider after the collision with the pellet?

Momentum

Momentum is a physical quantity that allows you to do calculations about what happens when moving bodies collide. You can use momentum to help you to analyse a car crash (Figure 15.3), the impact of a racket on a ball or, as above, a collision between an air-rifle pellet and an air track glider. (The momentum in this course is strictly called *linear* momentum, to distinguish it from the *angular* momentum of a spinning body.)

The **momentum** of a body is given by the word equation:

momentum = mass × velocity

or in symbols:

$$p = mv$$

You can see from the equations that the unit of momentum is the kg m s^{-1}.

Figure 15.3   The result of a collision

Momentum is a vector quantity; its direction is the same as that of the velocity of the body. The momentum of the snooker ball in Figure 15.4 is 0.6 kg m s^{-1} to the right. Figure 15.5 shows the ball after it has collided with the cushion. Its momentum is now 0.3 kg m s^{-1} to the left, which you could express as -0.3 kg m s^{-1} to the right.

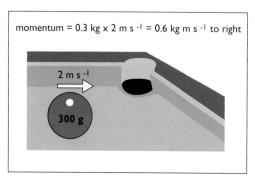

Figure 15.4   Momentum of snooker ball moving to right

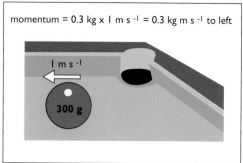

Figure 15.5   Momentum of snooker ball moving to left

Collisions on an air track

- Place two gliders of equal mass on an air track as shown in Figure 15.6. Give the left glider a push so that it collides and sticks to the right glider. The light gates measure the velocity of the left glider before the collision and of both gliders afterwards, by timing how long the card of known length takes to pass through the gates.
- Calculate the momentum of the left glider before the collision and the momentum of both gliders together afterwards.
- Repeat with different initial velocities and also vary the masses of the gliders involved.
- Extend your investigation to situations where the two gliders do not join together. In this case you will have to find the velocity of each glider separately after the collision. Remember that if the first glider moves to the left after the collision, then its velocity and momentum will be negative.

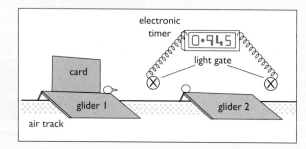

Figure 15.6   Investigating collisions on an air track

Collision between two bodies

If there are no external forces acting on a number of bodies, you find that momentum is conserved. This means that the total momentum after a collision is equal to the total momentum before the collision. This is the principle of **conservation of momentum**.

Worked example

A model railway truck of mass 2 kg moving at 5 m s^{-1} collides with another truck of mass 6 kg moving at 1 m s^{-1} in the same direction. If the two trucks join together, find their speed after the collision.

It is usually worth drawing a diagram of the situation, as in Figure 15.7. Then using the conservation of momentum,

initial momentum = final momentum

and using rightwards as positive, this is

$$(2 \text{ kg} \times 5 \text{ m s}^{-1}) + (6 \text{ kg} \times 1 \text{ m s}^{-1}) = 8 \text{ kg} \times v$$

$$10 \text{ kg m s}^{-1} + 6 \text{ kg m s}^{-1} = 8 \text{ kg} \times v$$

$$16 \text{ kg m s}^{-1} = 8 \text{ kg} \times v$$

$$v = 2 \text{ m s}^{-1}$$

So both trucks end up moving at 2 m s^{-1} to the right.

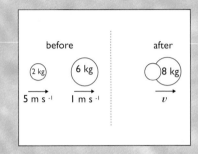

Figure 15.7 Before and after a collision

If the same collision happens, but this time the 6 kg truck bounces away from the collision at 3 m s^{-1} in the same direction, find the final speed of the 2 kg truck. Now look at Figure 15.8. Again

initial momentum = final momentum

and using rightwards as positive,

$$(2 \text{ kg} \times 5 \text{ m s}^{-1}) + (6 \text{ kg} \times 1 \text{ m s}^{-1}) = (2 \text{ kg} \times v) + (6 \text{ kg} \times 3 \text{ m s}^{-1})$$

$$16 \text{ kg m s}^{-1} = 2 \text{ kg} \times v + 18 \text{ kg m s}^{-1}$$

$$16 \text{ kg m s}^{-1} - 18 \text{ kg m s}^{-1} = 2 \text{ kg} \times v$$

$$-2 \text{ kg m s}^{-1} = 2 \text{ kg} \times v$$

$$v = -1 \text{ m s}^{-1}$$

This means that the 2 kg truck moves at 1 m s^{-1} to the left.

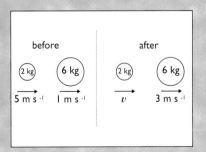

Figure 15.8 Before and after another collision

Change of momentum and impulse

Change of momentum

The momentum of the snooker ball in Figure 16.1 is 0.6 kg m s^{-1}. Its momentum in Figure 16.2, after colliding with the cushion, is -0.3 kg m s^{-1}. To calculate the change in momentum, as with any change, subtract the initial value from its final value. So

$$\text{change in momentum} = \text{final momentum} - \text{initial momentum}$$

In this case

$$\text{change of momentum} = (-0.3 \text{ kg m s}^{-1}) - (0.6 \text{ kg m s}^{-1})$$
$$= -0.9 \text{ kg m s}^{-1}$$

The change of momentum is negative, when rightwards is positive; this means that the change of momentum is to the left. The change of momentum of the snooker ball is caused by the force of the cushion on the ball during the collision.

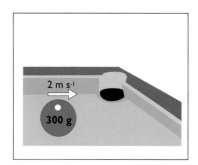

Figure 16.1 Snooker ball moving to right

Momentum and Newton's second law

In Chapter 7 you learned a statement of Newton's second law connecting force and acceleration. Newton himself expressed his second law in terms of momentum stating that:

> The rate of change of momentum of a body is directly proportional to the resultant force acting on it and takes place in the same direction as the resultant force.

This version of **Newton's second law** defines **force** to be the quantity which causes a rate of change of momentum. The larger the force, the larger the rate of change of momentum, or, if you prefer, the larger the change of momentum per second. The law also makes an important statement about direction. The rate of change of momentum is in the same direction as the force; that is, if the force is to the left, the rate of change of momentum is towards the left.

From this version of Newton's second law you can state:

$$\text{force} \propto \text{rate of change of momentum}$$

Since *rate of* means *divided by time*, and change = final − initial,

$$\text{force} \propto \frac{(\text{final momentum} - \text{initial momentum})}{\text{time}}$$

If the mass *m* is constant you can express this in symbols:

$$F \propto \frac{(mv - mu)}{t}$$

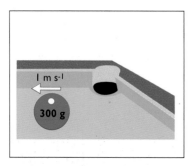

Figure 16.2 Snooker ball moving to left

where u and v are the initial and final velocities, and t is the time between these velocities.

In the International System of Units, the constant of proportionality is chosen to be 1. Therefore

$$F = \frac{(mv - mu)}{t}$$

$$F = \frac{m(v - u)}{t}$$

Since $(v_2 - v_1)/t$ is the acceleration a, we get

$$F = ma$$

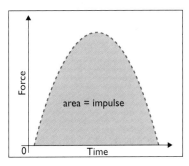

Figure 16.3 A large force changes the momentum of a golf ball in a short time

Impulse

The same change in momentum can be caused by a small force acting on a body for a long time, or a larger force acting on the body for a shorter time (Figure 16.3). Since

$$\text{force} = \frac{\text{change of momentum}}{\text{time}}$$

$$\text{force} \times \text{time} = \text{change of momentum}$$

Or in symbols,

$$Ft = mv - mu$$

The product force $\times$ time is the **impulse**; it is equal to the change of momentum. Impulse depends on both the size of the force and the time for which it acts.

It is easy to calculate the impulse of a steady force: simply multiply the force by the time for which it acts. If the force is changing steadily, multiply the average force by the time. If you have a graph of force against time, the impulse is equal to the area under the graph (Figure 16.4).

Since impulse is equal to change of momentum, the units of both must be the same: the kg m s^{-1}. You can see that the units of impulse are also the units of force $\times$ time, which is the N s. These are two different ways of saying the same thing, since

$$\text{N s} = \text{kg m s}^{-2} \times \text{s} = \text{kg m s}^{-1}$$

You can use this unit for both change of momentum and impulse. However, it is common practice to state impulse in N s and momentum in kg m s^{-1}.

Figure 16.5 is an example of a small (gravitational) force acting for a very long time.

Figure 16.4 The area under a force–time graph gives the impulse

Figure 16.5 A small gravitational force from the Sun, acting over a long time, gives the comet enormous momentum

Measuring the force of a kick

- Attach foil to both a football and the shoe of a kicker and use an electronic timer to measure the time they are in contact during a kick (Figure 16.6).
- Kick the ball horizontally. Measure the vertical distance fallen, the horizontal distance travelled and the duration of the kick.
- Measure the mass of the football and calculate the horizontal velocity of the ball as described in Chapter 5 (Practical: Measuring the speed of a snooker ball). Multiply mass by velocity to calculate the momentum given, and therefore the impulse applied to the ball.
- Divide the impulse by the time of contact to calculate the force applied.

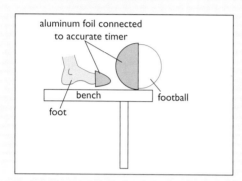

Figure 16.6   Measuring the contact time between ball and foot

Impulses in collisions

When two bodies collide, they exert equal and opposite forces on each other (Figure 16.7) and these Newton III pair of forces act for the same length of time.

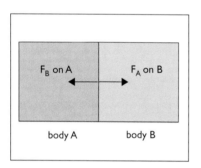

Figure 16.7   The forces between two colliding bodies

Since the times are equal and the forces are equal and opposite, the impulses are equal and opposite. Body A exerts on body B an equal and opposite impulse to that which body B exerts on body A. Therefore the change in the momentum of body B is equal and opposite to the change in the momentum of body A.

So the overall change in the total momentum of both bodies during the collision is zero; that is, momentum is conserved.

Explosions

When a crossbow shoots an arrow (Figure 16.8), the bow pushes the arrow forwards and the arrow pushes the bow backwards. Momentum is conserved. So the momentum gained in a forwards direction by the arrow is equal to the backward momentum that the arrow gives to the bow and whatever it is attached to.

When you fire an air-rifle (Figure 16.9), a sudden explosion pushes a pellet (and some gas) forwards at the same time as pushing the air-rifle backwards. The forward momentum that the explosion gives to pellet and gas is equal to the backward momentum that it gives to the air-rifle.

Figure 16.8   A bow firing an arrow

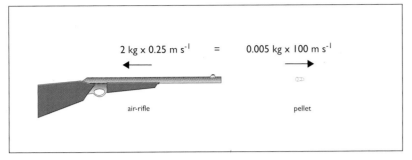

Figure 16.9 *If you hold the air-rifle so that it can move backwards freely, you can assume tht the momentum of the pellet is equal and opposite to that of the air-rifle*

Similarly, when bombs and shells explode, the increase in momentum in any one direction is matched by an increase in momentum in the opposite direction, so the total momentum is unchanged.

A rocket engine fires hot gases from its exhaust. As the engine pushes the gases backwards, the gases push the rocket forwards (Figure 16.10). Again, the increase in the momentum of the rocket forwards is equal to the increase in momentum of the exhaust gases backwards.

Figure 16.10 *European rocket launcher taking off*

Work, energy and power

Figure 17.1 Two methods of supporting the same load

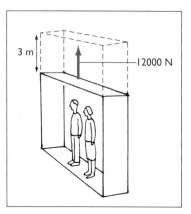

Figure 17.2 Raising this lift 3 m needs 36 000 J

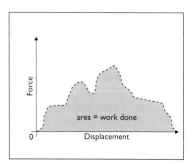

Figure 17.3 The area under a force–displacement graph gives the work done

Work

Many tasks involving force or motion are tiring. For instance, if you were supporting a heavy load you would get tired and need an input from your food. But you could be replaced by a shelf which would support the load without needing to be fed (Figure 17.1).

If a moving object were on a smooth surface, or in outer space, it would continue to move at a constant speed. It doesn't need an input to keep it going.

But there are many tasks that by their very nature do need an input. For instance, if you want to raise a load, or grind a mineral, or drill a hole, you need a person or animal that needs feeding, or something like an electric motor or a petrol-powered engine that needs electricity or fuel. Processes that need an input like this are what physicists call **work**. Work is done when a body exerts a force and moves a distance in the direction of the force:

work = force × displacement in the direction of the force

$$\Delta W = F \, \Delta x$$

A small bunch of keys may have a weight of about 1 N. If you raise them through a height of 1 m

$$\Delta W = F \, \Delta x = 1 \text{ N} \times 1 \text{ m} = 1 \text{ N m}$$

The unit of work is the newton metre (N m), called a joule (J).

Another example is shown in Figure 17.2.

If the force is changing steadily, you can calculate the work done by multiplying the average force by the displacement in the direction of the force. If you have a graph of force against displacement, the work done is the area under the graph (Figure 17.3).

Energy

Physicists use the word **system** to describe a body, or a group of bodies, that they are thinking about. Energy is a mathematical quantity which changes when work is done on, or by, a system (Figure 17.4). When a system does work, its energy decreases. When you do work on a system, its energy increases.

If you do work squashing a spring, your energy decreases, and the energy of the spring increases. If a battery-powered winch raises a load, then the energy of the battery decreases and the energy of the load increases.

If any system does an amount of work ΔW, then its energy decreases by an amount ΔW, and the energy of the system that it is working on increases by an amount ΔW. The amount of work done is equal to the amount of energy transferred from one system to another:

energy transferred = work done

So if you do 250 J of work squashing a spring, your energy decreases by 250 J and the energy of the spring increases by 250 J.

Power

The rate of doing work is called **power**. This is the same as the rate of energy transfer. You know that rate of means divided by time. So you can see that

$$\text{power} = \frac{\text{energy transfer}}{\text{time}} = \frac{\text{work}}{\text{time}}$$

In symbols,

$$\text{power} = \frac{\Delta E}{\Delta t} \quad \text{or} \quad \text{power} = \frac{\Delta W}{\Delta t}$$

where the use of the Δ symbols means that the times are short.

The unit of power is the joule per second or watt (W).

In the days when horsepower was important, it was reckoned that a horse could raise a weight of 500 N when moving 3 m in 2 s. The work done in 2 s is

$$F \, \Delta x = 500 \text{ N} \times 3 \text{ m} = 1500 \text{ J}$$

so that

$$\text{power} = \frac{\text{work}}{\text{time}} = \frac{1500 \text{ J}}{2 \text{ s}} = 750 \text{ W}$$

Here is another equation for power. Since power = work/time and work = force × displacement, then

$$\text{power} = \frac{\text{work}}{\text{time}} = \frac{\text{force x displacement}}{\text{time}} = \frac{\text{force} \times \text{displacement}}{\text{time}}$$

power = force × velocity

The horse above pulls a load of 500 N at a speed of 1.5 m s^{-1}. Its power is therefore 500 N × 1.5 m s^{-1} = 750 W.

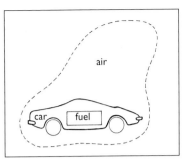

Figure 17.4 The car, fuel and air are a system that has energy

Measuring your power

- Measure your weight.
- Then time how long you take to run up a flight of stairs as quickly as you can.
- Measure the height of the flight (Figure 17.5) and calculate the work you did.
- Divide by the time to calculate your power.

Figure 17.5 Running upstairs

Potential and kinetic energy

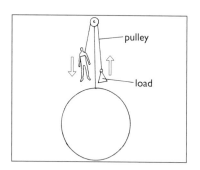

Figure 18.1 As you fall, you do work. The system containing you and the Earth loses energy

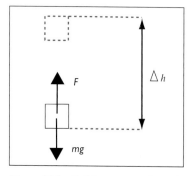

Figure 18.2 The falling mass does work and raises the energy of you and the Earth

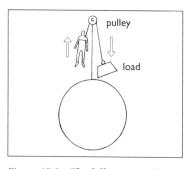

Figure 18.3 Raising a mass through a distance Δh

Systems that can do work

You can use the energy of many different types of system to do work. For example, a mixture of food and oxygen has energy that you can use to do work. A petrol–air mixture enables a car engine to do work; a coal–air mixture enables the turbines in a power station to do work. You can use moving bodies to do work, or hot bodies. High bodies can do work; so can squashed springs and nuclear fuels. All these systems have energy, and since they are different, it is tempting to give the energy in them all different names. But when you study energy in detail, you find that there are really only two different ways of storing energy, as *potential* energy or as *kinetic* energy.

Gravitational potential energy

Think about yourself and the Earth as a system. There are gravitational forces between you and the Earth. If you are separated from the Earth, the Earth pulls you down again, and this can do work, for instance by raising a load (Figure 18.1).

If, on the other hand, the load raises you, it does work on you, separating you from the Earth and increasing the energy of your system (Figure 18.2).

If you are high, you have energy. If the load is high, it has energy. In both cases the energy is the consequence of the *position* of a body on which *forces* act. Energy stored like this is called *potential* energy. In this case the forces are gravitational, so the energy is **gravitational potential energy**.

Electromagnetic and nuclear potential energy

Potential energy is also associated with electromagnetic and nuclear forces. If you stretch a spring, you distort the electrostatic bonds between the atoms, and the spring has electromagnetic potential energy, though we often refer to this as elastic potential energy.

Electromagnetic potential energy depends on the arrangement of charges. It is responsible for the energy stored in batteries, capacitors, two magnets squashed together, food plus oxygen, fuel plus oxygen and squashed-up springs and energy released in chemical reactions.

Nuclear fuels have potential energy as a consequence of the strong and weak forces within the nucleus.

Calculating potential energy

The force needed to raise a mass m in a gravitational field g at constant speed is mg. The work done in raising this mass (Figure 18.3) through a height Δh is

$$\Delta W = \text{force} \times \text{displacement} = mg\Delta h$$

This is the increase in gravitational potential energy.

Figure 18.4 shows a force–extension graph for a spring. You know from Chapter 17 that the work done is the area under the graph. This is the area of the shaded triangle. This equals the amount of elastic potential energy stored in the spring.

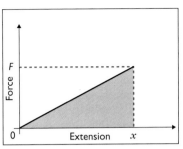

Figure 18.4   Energy stored in spring = area of triangle = $\frac{1}{2}Fx$

Kinetic energy

You need to do work on a body to get it moving. When it is moving, it has energy – known as **kinetic energy** – and you can use this energy to do work.

You can calculate how much kinetic energy a body has from the amount of work you need to get it moving. When a constant resultant force F accelerates a body of mass m from rest to a velocity v, the work done appears as kinetic energy of the moving body (Figure 18.5). If the acceleration occurs over a distance x then

$$\text{work done} = Fx$$

Since $F = ma$,

$$Fx = max$$

But $v^2 = u^2 + 2ax$, and since $u = 0$, $ax = \frac{1}{2}v^2$,

$$\text{work done} = Fx = max = m(\tfrac{1}{2}v^2) = \tfrac{1}{2}mv^2$$

$$\text{kinetic energy} = \tfrac{1}{2}mv^2$$

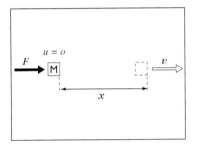

Figure 18.5   Work done in accelerating a mass appears as kinetic energy

Measuring the energy stored in a rubber band

- Take measurements and plot a force–extension graph for the rubber band.
- Use the band to catapult the glider along the air track (Figure 18.6). Measure the extension and use the light gate and card to measure the speed of the glider.
- Use the graph to calculate the energy released by the band and compare this with the kinetic energy of the glider.
- Repeat for a range of extensions.

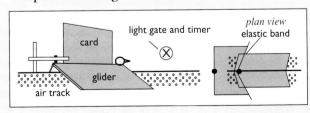

Figure 18.6   Catapulting an air track glider using an elastic band

19 | Conservation of energy

Measuring potential energy and kinetic energy

- Set up the apparatus as in Figure 19.1. As the mass falls and loses potential energy, both the mass and the glider gain kinetic energy.
- Calculate the potential energy lost by the mass in pulling the glider to the light gate. Use the light gate and card to measure the speed of the mass and glider and calculate the kinetic energy they gain.
- Compare the potential energy lost with the kinetic energy gained.
- Repeat using different masses and release heights.

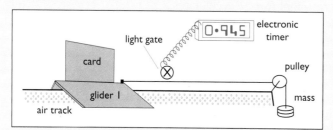

Figure 19.1   Using a falling mass to accelerate an air track glider

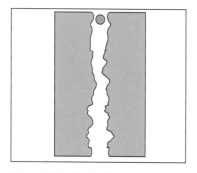

Figure 19.2   The ball gains very little kinetic energy as it falls through a rough tube

Figure 19.3   The mud ball loses kinetic energy as it hits the wall

Gain and loss of energy

If the air track and pulley in Figure 19.1 are very smooth, the kinetic energy gained by the glider and mass is very nearly equal to the potential energy lost by the mass falling. Of course the connecting string and pulley gain some energy. If you calculate their kinetic energy as well, then you find that the potential energy lost by the mass is even more closely equal to the kinetic energy of the moving parts. In experiments like this, where there is an exchange between potential energy and kinetic energy, you seem to end up with the same amount of energy at the end as you had in the beginning.

Internal energy

It is very easy, however, to think of situations in which potential energy or kinetic energy seems to be lost without a corresponding gain elsewhere.

The mass in Figure 19.2 loses potential energy as it falls through the very rough tube but does not gain much kinetic energy.

The ball of mud in Figure 19.3 loses kinetic energy when it hits the wall but nothing seems to gain potential energy.

Observations like these do not seem to fit in with experiments that seem to show that, whenever there is a loss of energy somewhere, there is a gain elsewhere. These observations were a puzzle for scientists for a long time until they noticed that, in such situations where there is a loss of potential and kinetic energy, the temperature of the bodies involved always increases.

The molecules in bodies are in a continuous state of random motion. They have random kinetic energy. The molecules have electromagnetic forces between them and when they move relative to one another these are stores of random potential energy.

When the ball runs down the rough tube, its potential energy is used to give its own molecules and those of the tube more random kinetic and potential energy. You notice this by the increase in temperature of the ball and the tube. Similarly the temperatures of the mud ball and wall both rise when the ball hits the wall.

The random kinetic and potential energy of the molecules of a body are known as **internal energy**. Internal energy is sometimes referred to as thermal energy or, improperly, as heat. You will find out in Module 3 how to calculate the internal energy gained by a body.

Conservation of energy

Careful measurements with many experiments, together with much indirect evidence, has led physicists to state the principle of **conservation of energy**. This states that, in any system isolated from its surroundings, the total amount of energy in that system remains constant. The energy may move about or be rearranged within that system, but there is no increase or decrease; energy is neither created nor destroyed.

Efficiency

When you walk about or run upstairs, you do work. To do this work you need energy released as your food combines with oxygen from the air. The energy you need is always more than the work you do. No energy is lost; you don't put out less energy than you take in. It is just that you don't use all the energy you take in to do work moving about or raising yourself up.

This is true for almost any process that any machine, engine or mechanical device undertakes. The useful output is never greater than the input, and it is almost always less than the input. For efficient devices, less of the input is wasted and a bigger proportion is useful output.

We define **efficiency** as the proportion of the work or energy input that comes out usefully:

$$\text{efficiency} = \frac{\text{useful output}}{\text{input}}$$

The efficiency of systems varies over a wide range. A manual car gear box is well over 95 per cent efficient; a car engine is less than 40 per cent efficient. You can read more about engine efficiency in the text for Module 3.

Elastic and inelastic collisions

Investigating collisions

- Use spring buffers on the gliders as in Figure 20.1. Send them towards each other so that they collide gently and bounce off each other.
- Find the total kinetic energy before the collision and afterwards. Repeat for a range of speeds.
- Replace the spring buffers with Plasticine so that the gliders stick together after colliding.
- Again determine the kinetic energy before and after the collision.

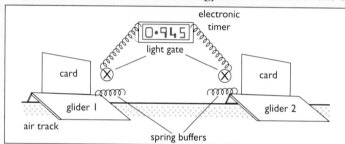

Figure 20.1   Two gliders on an air track before collision

Types of collision

You know that, in all collisions in systems which are isolated from their surroundings, both momentum and energy are conserved. There are some collisions in which kinetic energy seems to be conserved, and some in which it clearly is not.

If gliders on an air track have very springy buffers, there is no loss of kinetic energy when they collide. These are **elastic collisions**. If the buffers are not springy, for instance if they are made of Plasticine, then there are losses of kinetic energy when the gliders collide. These are **inelastic collisions**. Very few collisions between bodies are completely elastic, since there is a general tendency for kinetic energy to be lost as bodies interact and for this to increase the amount of internal energy.

This trend, from the ordered kinetic and potential energy of bodies to the disordered internal energy inside bodies, is part of the general trend to disorder in the universe. There is more about this subject in the text for Module 3.

Collisions between the molecules of gases are, on average, elastic. If this were not so, the molecules would gradually slow down and sink to the bottom of the container they were in.

The simple pendulum

In a freely swinging pendulum (Figure 20.2) there is a constant interchange between gravitational potential energy and kinetic energy and back. At the centre the bob is at its lowest point and has minimum gravitational potential energy and maximum kinetic energy. It is at this point that it is moving at its maximum speed. At the extreme positions the bob is momentarily at rest; it has zero kinetic energy and maximum gravitational potential energy. The effects of friction on a heavy bob are very small over a single oscillation, but the small frictional forces have an effect in the long term. Energy gradually leaks from the pendulum and the internal energy of the surroundings increases.

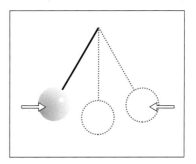

Figure 20.2   The motion of a simple pendulum

Using a ballistic pendulum to measure the speed of an air rifle pellet

- Find the mass of a pellet and the mass of the Plasticine bob. Fire the pellet horizontally so that it embeds in the suspended Plasticine (Figure 20.3).
- Record the maximum height h that the bob rises during its swing (Figure 20.4). Calculate the gravitational potential energy the bob and the pellet gain rising to the highest point. This is equal to the kinetic energy of bob and pellet after the impact. From this calculate the velocity of the bob and pellet just after impact, and their momentum.
- Use the law of conservation of momentum to obtain the initial momentum of the pellet and calculate the initial velocity of the pellet.
- Compare this answer with those you obtained by the methods in Chapter 15. Which of the three methods do you think is the most accurate?
- How does the initial kinetic energy of the pellet compare with the kinetic energy of the bob and pellet after impact? Account for any difference you observe.

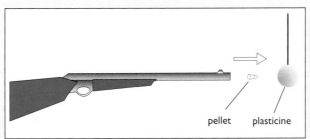

Figure 20.3   The pellet is about to enter the suspended Plasticine

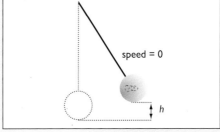

Figure 20.4   What is the maximum height of the pellet and Plasticine after impact?

When the pellet from the air rifle hits the Plasticine pendulum bob, the collision is inelastic. Most of the pellet's energy is used to change the shape of the Plasticine and thereby increase its internal energy. Modern cars are designed with a crumple zone at each end (Figure 20.5) which will change shape during impact and absorb the kinetic energy of the vehicle.

Figure 20.5   The crumple zone absorbs the kinetic energy of the car in a collision

Uniform circular motion

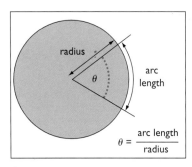

Figure 21.1 Measuring an angle in radians

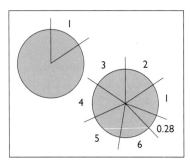

Figure 21.2 One radian is equal to 57°, and there are 6.28 radians in a circle

Figure 21.3 Circular motion can be fun!

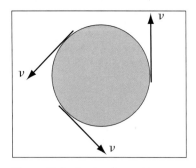

Figure 21.4 In circular motion, velocities are tangential

Changing direction

You know of many things that travel in circular paths. You may sit on a roundabout, follow a circular road, stand on the moving surface of the Earth. The path of the Moon around the Earth is nearly circular, as are the paths of the planets around the Sun. If a body moves along a circular path at constant speed it is performing uniform circular motion.

To study circular motion, you need to be able to use **radians** to measure angles. To find the size of an angle in radians, draw a circle centred on the apex of the angle and divide the length of the arc by the radius (Figure 21.1). One radian is just over 57°. As Figure 21.2 shows, there are $2\pi = 6.28$ radians in a whole circle.

The speed of a body in uniform circular motion is constant. But, as Figure 21.4 shows, its direction of motion is continually changing.

The body's velocity is a vector quantity and depends on direction. The direction is continuously changing, so the velocity of the body is continuously changing. If the velocity is changing, the body must be accelerating. But in this case the acceleration does not show that there is a change in the *magnitude* of the velocity (the speed), only its direction. Remember that acceleration is rate of change of velocity, not rate of change of speed. Since the body is accelerating, there must be a force acting on it to provide this acceleration.

Centripetal acceleration and force

The acceleration causes no increase in the speed. This is because it is at right angles to the velocity, towards the centre of the circle. This is **centripetal acceleration** (centripetal means centre-seeking). You may like to read Figure 21.5, which shows why the magnitude of the acceleration is given by v^2/r, where v and r are the speed of the body and the radius of the path.

The force causing the acceleration is towards the centre as well. It is called a **centripetal force**. Force = mass × acceleration, so for a body doing circular motion,

$$F = m\left(\frac{v^2}{r}\right) = \frac{mv^2}{r}$$

With circular motion, there is both force and motion, but the kinetic energy of the body does not change. So the resultant force is not doing any work on the body. The force and acceleration are towards the centre (Figure 21.6), but the velocity is at right angles to these. The distance moved in the direction of the force is zero.

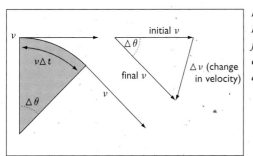

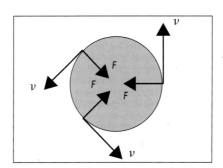

Figure 21.5 Derivation of formula for centripetal acceleration

Figure 21.6 In circular motion, forces act towards the centre of the circle

Testing the centripetal force equation

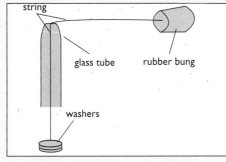

Figure 21.7 Testing the centripetal force equation

- Measure the mass of the bung. Put a mark on the string 2 m from the bung; thread the string through the glass tube and put a weight of 0.5 N on the other end.
- Hold the glass tube and swing the bung around in a horizontal circle (Figure 21.7) until the string lifts the weight and the circle has a radius of 2 m.
- Find the time for one rotation and use this to calculate the speed of the bung.
- Compare the centripetal force given by mv^2/r with the force of 0.5 N provided by the weight.
- Repeat with different weights and different radii.

Period and frequency

The **period** T of a body doing uniform circular motion is the time it takes to complete one revolution. Period is usually measured in seconds.

The **frequency** of rotation is the number of rotations per second. Frequency = 1/period; $f = 1/T$. The unit of frequency is s^{-1}, called the hertz (Hz).

Worked example

The rate of rotation of a compact disc varies, but a typical value is 78 revolutions per minute. So

$$\text{so period} = \frac{60 \text{ s}}{78} = 0.77 \text{ s and frequency} = \frac{1}{T} = \frac{1}{0.77} = 1.3 \text{ Hz}$$

angular velocity (see below)

$$\omega = 2\pi/T = 2\pi/0.77 = 8.2 \text{ rad s}^{-1}$$

Angular velocity

The **angular velocity** ω of a body is the central angle through which it turns in a second (Figure 21.8):

$$\omega = \theta/t$$

It takes a time T for a body to complete one revolution about the centre. During this time the body rotates through an angle of 2π radians about the centre. So

$$\omega = \frac{\theta}{t} = \frac{2\pi}{T} \qquad \text{Since } T = \frac{1}{f}, \qquad \omega = \frac{2\pi}{(1/f)} = 2\pi f$$

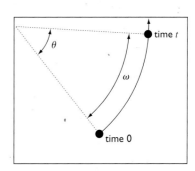

Figure 21.8 Angular velocity $\omega = \theta/t$

Calculating force and acceleration from ω

When a body is doing uniform circular motion, it travels right round the circumference, a distance $2\pi r$, in a time T. You know that speed = distance/time, so

$$v = \frac{2\pi r}{T}$$

But $T = 2\pi/\omega$, so

$$v = \frac{2\pi r}{(2\pi/\omega)}$$

$$v = r\omega$$

You know that centripetal acceleration $a = v^2/r$. So

$$a = (r^2\omega^2)^2/r = r\omega^2$$

and

$$\text{centripetal force} = ma = mr\omega^2$$

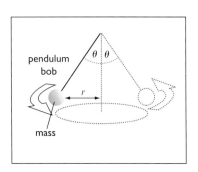

Figure 21.9   A conical pendulum

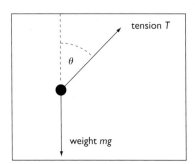

Figure 21.10   Free-body force diagram for the bob

The conical pendulum

Figure 21.9 shows a conical pendulum. The bob is moving at a constant speed in a horizontal circle. There are two forces acting on the bob: its weight and the tension in the string (Figure 21.10). The circle is horizontal, so there is no vertical motion; the bob is in vertical equilibrium. Therefore the vertical component of the tension equals the weight of the bob:

$$T \cos \theta = mg$$

The circular motion requires a resultant horizontal force towards the centre. The horizontal component of the tension provides this:

$$T \sin \theta = mv^2/r$$

Combining these two expressions gives

$$\frac{T \sin \theta}{T \cos \theta} = \frac{(mv^2)}{r} \frac{1}{mg}$$

$$\tan \theta = v^2/rg$$

If a conical pendulum is swinging in a horizontal circle of radius 1.5 m at an angle of 10° to the vertical, numerically

$$v^2 = rg \tan \theta = 1.5 \text{ m} \times 9.8 \text{ m s}^{-2} \times \tan(10°)$$

$$v^2 = 2.59 \text{ m}^2 \text{ s}^{-2}$$

$$v = 1.6 \text{ m s}^{-1}$$

Circular motion under gravity

Whirling a bung

- Observe the forcemeter as you whirl the bung in a vertical circle (Figure 22.1).
- Whirl the bung quickly, then as slowly as you can whilst still keeping it moving in a circle. You will not be able to make it move at constant speed in a circular path, but do your best.
- When the bung is moving slowly, notice how the tension varies around the circle.

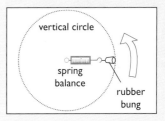

Figure 22.1 Forcemeter used to monitor tension in string

Motion in a vertical circle

When a body is moving at constant speed in a vertical circle, the centripetal acceleration is the same size at all positions around the circle and always directed towards the centre. So the resultant force on the body, the centripetal force, also has the same size and is directed towards the centre of the circle (Figure 22.2).

If you swing a bung round vertically, the centripetal force is provided by the resultant of two forces—the force of the string and the force of gravity.

At point C in the Figure 22.2 the string is pulling towards the centre, and the weight is pulling away from the centre (Figure 22.3). The string has to support the weight of the body as well as providing the upward centripetal force acting on it. The tension is at its greatest at this point.

At point A the weight of the body is providing some of the downward centripetal force (Figure 22.4). The string has only to provide the remainder. The tension is at its smallest at this point. As you reduce the speed of rotation, there comes a time when the weight alone is sufficient to provide the centripetal force. At that speed, the tension drops to zero at the top.

Loop-the-loop rides

Look at the ride shown in Figure 22.5. At the bottom of the loop, the upward contact force from the track equals the weight of the vehicle plus the required centripetal force. At the top, the track and the weight together provide the centripetal force. If the speed is slow enough at the top, the weight alone is exactly the required centripetal force and the track no longer exerts any force on the vehicle and its passengers. Indeed, you could remove a small section of track at the top, and the vehicle would continue unaffected, falling freely, but still following the circular path.

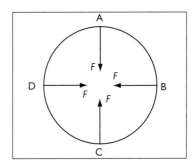

Figure 22.2 Required centripetal force has constant magnitude

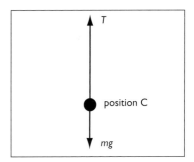

Figure 22.3 Resultant provides upward centripetal force

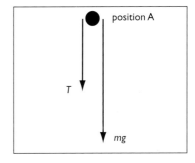

Figure 22.4 Resultant provides downward centripetal force of same magnitude

Figure 22.5   People enjoying themselves on a loop-the-loop ride!

Figure 22.6   If you jump off a high diving board, you experience apparent weightlessness

Weightlessness and apparent weightlessness

Figure 13.3 showed how gravity produces tensions and compressions in parts of your body. These give you the experience of having a weight. If you are a long way from all other masses, you would be **weightless**. You would feel weightless because you would no longer feel the tensions and compressions that weight produces.

If you fall freely, for instance if you jump off a high diving board (Figure 22.6), the downwards gravitational forces are still there but there are no supporting forces. All parts of your body accelerate downwards at a rate equal to g. The lack of upwards forces means that the normal tensions and compressions are not there, so it feels as if you are weightless. This is **apparent weightlessness**.

If you go over a loop-the-loop ride where the only force acting on you at the top is weight, again you would feel weightless as you fall freely towards the Earth.

An astronaut in an orbiting spacecraft (Figure 22.7) is falling freely towards the Earth. His weight is the centripetal force for his circular motion, and there are no supporting forces. Though he has a weight, he feels weightless.

Figure 22.7   An astronaut 'floating' inside a spacecraft

Electricity

An example of 25 kV at 200 A

What happens in an electric circuit?

Lighting a lamp

- Connect a lamp to a cell (Figure 23.1). Observe what happens.
- What will happen if the lamp is connected to the cell for a long time?
- Predict what will happen if you connect a battery of two cells to the lamp (Figure 23.2). Then test your prediction.
- Repeat with three cells.

Figure 23.1   Energy is transferred from the cell to the lamp

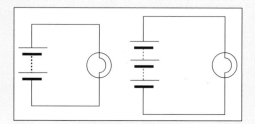

Figure 23.2   Two cells and three cells in series

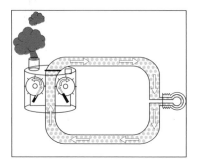

Figure 23.3   A mechanical analogy—the engine pushes the balls around the 'circuit'

Energy from cell to lamp

Figure 23.1 shows a cell connected to a lamp. The lamp filament gets hot, perhaps hot enough to emit light. Energy is transferred from the cell to the lamp; the lamp gains energy from the cell and the cell loses energy to the lamp. Eventually the cell runs down and the lamp goes out.

Like any electrical circuit, Figure 23.1 has a power source (the cell) and a complete circuit. The fact that you need a complete circuit for electrical circuits to work suggests that something is flowing, going into components through one lead and out through the other.

A mechanical analogy

Figure 23.3 shows a similar mechanical situation. The engine pushes balls through a pipe. The balls are like whatever flows round an electrical circuit, and the engine is like whatever does the pushing. The balls flow through the pipe, through the lamp and eventually back to the engine. Where they have to move more quickly through the thin part of the circuit in the lamp they make the pipe hot. Eventually the engine runs out of fuel; it no longer pushes, and the flow stops.

Charge carriers

In an electrical circuit, the balls that move are very small and are called **charge carriers**. The 'engine' that pushes them is the chemical reaction in the **cells**. The flow of charge is called a **current**, and it is common to put an arrow on circuits from the part of the supply labelled positive, through the external circuit and back to the part of the cell labelled negative, to show the direction of the current (Figure 23.4).

In most circuits, the charge carriers are electrons, which flow round the circuit from the negative of the cell to the positive, in the opposite direction from the current arrows. But the practical effect is just like pushing positive charge carriers around.

Electrical work

The cell in the circuit applies a force to the charge carriers in the direction in which they move; it works on the charge carriers. In turn, the charge carriers work on the lamp filament. Electrical work is very similar to mechanical work, but it is invisible. You can detect it only by its effects. When electrical work is done, energy is being transferred.

More cells and more lamps

A group of cells connected together is called a **battery**. Some are shown in Figure 23.5. If you connect a battery of two cells in series to the lamp, the lamp shines more brightly. Both cells push the electrons; the electrons move faster (Figure 23.6). The bigger current makes the lamp brighter.

But if you connect a single cell to two lamps like in Figure 23.7, then the electrons will slow down. There is the same push, but both lamps resist the movement of the electrons.

Direct current (d.c.) and alternating current (a.c.)

In the circuits mentioned so far, the cells push the electrons in one direction only and the electrons travel in this direction. This is **direct current**.

An alternating current power supply pushes the electrons first one way and then the other. The electrons in the circuit move backwards and forwards. The power supply still supplies energy but without the electrons moving steadily in any one direction. The electrons move equally in both directions; they take part in transferring energy from supply to the load, but they never go from one to the other themselves.

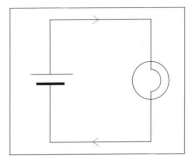

Figure 23.4 Arrows indicate the direction of the current

Figure 23.5 Alkaline, Leclanché and rechargeable nickel–cadmium cells and 9 V zinc–carbon battery

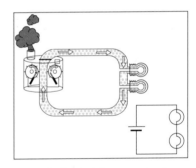

Figure 23.7 Both lamps resist the current, so the flow is less

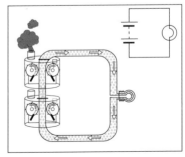

Figure 23.6 With two cells (engines), the electrons (balls) move faster

24 Charge and current

Polythene strip

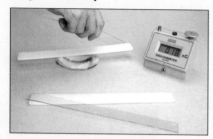

Figure 24.1 Investigating charge

- Rub a polythene strip with a duster, and then balance it on an upturned watch glass (Figure 24.1).
- Rub another polythene strip and hold the rubbed end near the rubbed end of the strip on the watch glass. What do you notice?
- Repeat with two acetate strips; then with one acetate strip and one polythene strip.
- Rub the strips again and scrape them on the coulombmeter plate and note the readings.

Charge

Atoms are mainly protons, neutrons and electrons. Protons and electrons both have **charge**—the property that gives rise to the electrical forces mentioned in Chapter 9. The charge on the electron is called negative, and that on the proton is called positive. Most things, most of the time, have equal numbers of protons and electrons. The charges cancel out and so you do not notice electrical effects. The objects are uncharged or **neutral**. The neutron is neutral.

Electrons are on the outsides of atoms, so they can be moved around. Generally, when you observe electrical effects, it is because electrons have moved around.

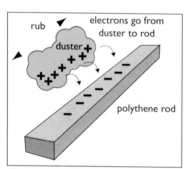

Figure 24.2 Charging a polythene rod

Unequal charges

When you rub a neutral polythene rod with a duster, you transfer electrons from the duster to the rod (Figure 24.2), giving the polythene a surplus of electrons and making it negative. The rod will repel another rubbed polythene rod, because *like charges repel*.

When you rub an acetate rod, electrons go from the rod to the duster (Figure 24.3). The acetate is short of electrons, and therefore positive. An acetate rod will attract a polythene rod because *unlike charges attract*.

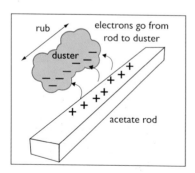

Figure 24.3 Charging an acetate rod

Measuring charge

Since electrons and protons have the same size of charge, you could measure charge in 'electrons worth'. But the charge on an electron is much too small for everyday use as a unit. So the **coulomb** is used. The charge on one electron is 1.6×10^{-19} C. So one coulomb (1 C) is the charge carried by about 6.25×10^{18} electrons. Coulombmeters measure charge and show whether it is positive or negative. They usually measure in nanocoulombs (1 nC = 10^{-9} C), which is the charge carried by 6 250 000 000 electrons. A charged polythene rod may have a charge of hundreds of nanocoulombs, so you can see that vast numbers of electrons move around when you charge a plastic rod.

Discharging a coulombmeter

Figure 24.4   Discharging a coulombmeter

- A coulombmeter stores the charge it measures.
- Charge a coulombmeter with a polythene rod to at least −1000 nC.
- Then discharge it by connecting a microammeter to it as shown.
- Observe the microammeter as the coulombmeter discharges (Figure 24.4).

Moving charge

While the coulombmeter discharges through the microammeter, the extra electrons, which are transferred to the coulombmeter plate while you charge it, run to the other terminal through the microammeter. The microammeter shows a current. This shows that while charge moves you get a current.

Charging a coulombmeter with a known current

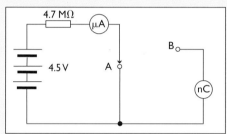

Figure 24.5   Charging a coulombmeter

- Set up the circuit shown in Figure 24.5.
- Check that the ammeter reads a current of about 1 µA when it is connected to A.
- Zero the coulombmeter and then connect the ammeter to B. Watch what happens.
- Zero the coulombmeter again and measure the charge that flows when a current of 1 µA flows for 1 s.

Calculating charge

The **current** is the rate of flow of charge, that is, the quantity of charge that flows per second. Current is measured in amperes. One ampere (1 A) is equal to one coulomb per second (1 C s^{-1}). When a charge of 1 C flows past a point in 1 s, the current is 1 coulomb per second, that is 1 A. When a charge of 1 µC flows in 1 s, the current is 1 µA. We can write

current = rate of flow of charge

$$I = \frac{\Delta Q}{\Delta t}$$

where I is the current and ΔQ is the charge that flows in a time Δt.

The equation $\Delta Q = I \Delta t$ defines the derived quantity of charge from the base quantities of current and time.

Charge and batteries

An ordinary D-size battery can supply 0.3 A for 4 h. This means its capacity is 0.3 A × 4 h = 1.2 A h. It will supply a current of 1.2 A for 1 h, or 0.12 A for 10 h, etc. You can calculate the charge that moves during the lifetime of the battery from these figures. You know that

$$I = \frac{\Delta Q}{\Delta t} \text{ so } \Delta Q = I \Delta t = 0.3 \text{ A} \times (4 \times 3600) \text{ s} = 4320 \text{ C}$$

Two examples are shown in Figures 24.6 and 24.7. Calculate the charge that moves in each case.

Figure 24.6   A hearing-aid battery will supply 10 µA continuously for 6 months

Figure 24.7   A car battery with a capacity of 24 A h

Current in series circuits

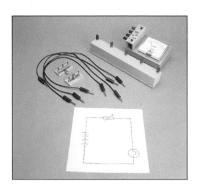

Figure 25.1   *The circuit diagram and some components*

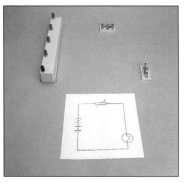

Figure 25.2   *Components laid out as in circuit diagram*

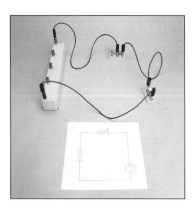

Figure 25.3   *Components connected with leads to have correct arrangement*

Setting up circuits

Learn the good habit of laying out your circuits neatly and carefully, even with simple circuits. It makes understanding them and finding faults so much easier.

First put a copy of the circuit diagram (Figure 25.1) directly in front of you, so that you can compare the circuit diagram with the component layout. If you are stuck, make the copy big and put the components on top of the diagram.

Position the components in exactly the same way as they are shown in the circuit diagram (Figure 25.2).

Finally, connect the components using leads of the right length to keep the circuit looking just like the circuit diagram (Figure 25.3).

Using ammeters

You use an ammeter to find the current flowing through a particular point in a circuit.

First set up the circuit and decide where you wish to measure the current. Then break the circuit at the required point (Figure 25.4).

Finally insert the ammeter (Figure 25.5). You should usually only need a single extra lead. You can then read the meter.

The ammeter deflects in the correct direction if its red terminal is connected nearest to the positive terminal of the power supply. But if the reading is negative, just reverse the connections.

Reading meter scales

Take care when you read meter scales because the numbers on them may not correspond exactly to the values measured.

The meter in Figure 25.6 is measuring the current through the lamp. It uses a 100 mA adapter, called a **shunt**, which allows it to measure up to 100 mA maximum. The shunt is 100 mA f.s.d., which means 100 mA full-scale deflection. This means that when the meter is at full-scale deflection (at its maximum positive reading), the current through the instrument is 100 mA.

There are two scales on the meter. In this case, the top one is the easiest to use, since 10 on the top scale corresponds to 100 mA. So calculate the current that is flowing through the meter by multiplying the top scale reading by 10 mA. The current in this case is 65 mA.

With a 500 mA shunt, use the bottom scale and multiply its reading by 100 mA.

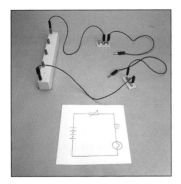

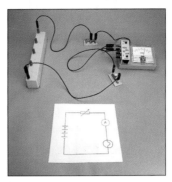

Figure 25.4   Circuit broken at point where you want to measure the current

Figure 25.5   Circuit completed with ammeter

Figure 25.6   What is the current through this meter?

Measuring the current in a series circuit

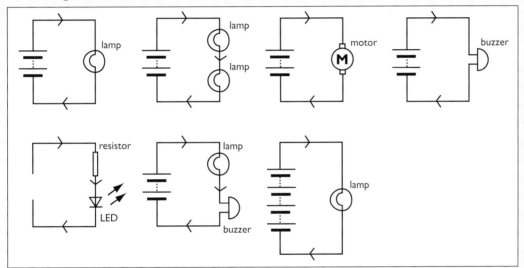

Figure 25.7   Series circuits

- Set up the circuits in Figure 25.7 and use an ammeter to measure the current through every accessible wire in the circuit.
- When you have done one or two measurements, predict what your readings will be before taking the remaining measurements.

What happens in a series circuit?

The circuits in Figure 25.7 are all examples of **series** circuits. The current passes through one component, then through the next, and then through the next, etc. When components are in series, the current through each is the same. The number of electrons that go into a component in each second is the same as the number that come out the other end. Charge and current are not used up by the component: what goes in comes out.

If you think back to the engine diagrams in Chapter 23, this might help you to understand what is going on. The number of balls per second going into any component is equal to the number coming out per second.

How fast does charge move?

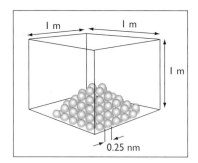

Figure 26.1 A cubical array of copper atoms

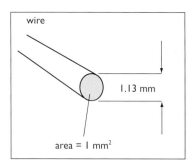

Figure 26.2 The wire has a cross-sectional area of 1 mm²

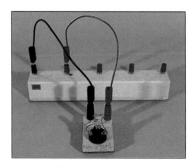

Figure 26.3 A torch bulb carries a current of about 0.2 A

Free charge in a conductor

Most of the electrons in metallic conductors are fixed to their atoms, but for each atom, one or two electrons are free to move and carry charge. If you calculate how many atoms there are in a cubic metre, you can estimate the number of free electrons per cubic metre.

The atoms in copper have a diameter of about 0.25 nm. Assume that they are stacked together cubically, as shown in Figure 26.1. There will be 1 m/0.25 nm = 4×10^9 atoms along each edge of a one-metre cube. Therefore there will be $(4 \times 10^9)^3 = 6.4 \times 10^{28}$ atoms in a cubic metre. Assuming one free electron per atom, this gives a figure of about 6.4×10^{28} electrons per metre cubed. This is known as the **charge carrier density** or just as the **carrier density**. It has the symbol n.

The free charge in a metre cubed is therefore about $6.4 \times 10^{28} \times 1.6 \times 10^{-19} = 1.0 \times 10^{10}$ coulomb, so in a piece of copper 1 mm³, there are 10 C of free charge.

How fast does charge move?

Electrical effects happen very quickly. A lamp seems to light almost instantly when you connect it to a power supply, even if the leads are very long. It makes it interesting to consider how quickly the charge flows. A typical copper connecting wire (Figure 26.2) has a cross-sectional area of 1 mm². If free electrons in the wire move at 1 millimetre per second, then 1 mm³ of electrons pass a point each second. From the paragraph above, you know that this corresponds to a charge of 10 coulombs flowing, and if 10 C flow past a point in a second, the current is 10 A.

A small torch bulb may take a current of 0.2 A (Figure 26.3), which is 1/50th of 10 A. So the charge must be moving at 1/50th of the speed that it would do in a wire carrying 10 A, which is 1/50th millimetre per second. How can this slow charge speed be compatible with a lamp lighting nearly as soon as you turn it on?

Why so fast, when the charge moves so slowly?

When you turn a circuit on, electrons throughout the circuit start moving almost straight away. It is rather like pushing balls through a tube. As soon as a ball goes in to one end of a tube another ball comes out of the far end (Figure 26.4). It isn't necessary for the ball to get from one end to the other before the effects are evident at the far end.

Electrical effects are not quite instantaneous. The information that starts the electrons moving travels around the circuit at the speed of light in the form of an electromagnetic wave; so electrical effects travel at the speed of light.

Calculating the speed of charge movement

The wire shown in Figure 26.5 has a charge carrier density n, each carrier having charge q and moving at speed v (called the **drift speed**). The wire has a cross-sectional area A and the current through it is I.

The volume of charge carriers passing a point in one second is Av.
So the number of charge carriers passing a point in one second is nAv.
But

current = charge past a point in one second = $nAvq$

Therefore

$I = nAqv$

You can use this formula to calculate the drift speed of electrons in a copper wire of cross-sectional area 1 mm², carrying a current of 0.2 A. Rearranging it gives

$v = I/nAq$

$= 0.2 \text{ A} / (6.4 \times 10^{28} \text{ m}^{-3} \times 1 \times 10^{-6} \text{ m}^2 \times 1.6 \times 10^{-19} \text{ C})$

$= 0.02 \text{ mm s}^{-1}$

This is the same figure as was calculated earlier. This speed is a typical speed for electrons travelling in a conductor. Imagine how slow it is. It is tiny compared with the random motion that the electrons have irrespective of the current that they are carrying. Chapter 33 discusses the motion of charge carriers in more detail.

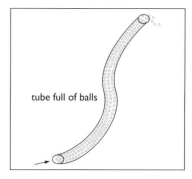

Figure 26.4   As soon as you push a ball into one end, a ball comes out of the other

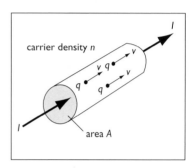

Figure 26.5   A wire carrying a current

Conduction by coloured salts

- Some chemicals have coloured ions that you can see moving in solution.
- Connect up the apparatus as in Figure 26.6. Wet the filter paper with ammonium solution and put on a single crystal of copper sulphate and a single crystal of potassium permanganate.
- Observe the speed of movement of the ions.
- The copper ion is blue and the permanganate ion is purple. What can you deduce about the charges on the ions?

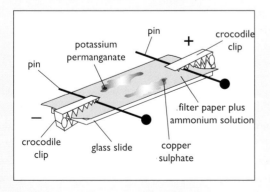

Figure 26.6   You can see coloured manganate and copper ions moving

Kirchhoff's first law

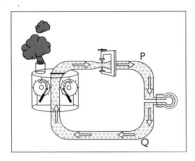

Figure 27.1   If the pipe is squashed, the current is reduced

Reducing the flow

Consider the effect of an obstruction in a mechanical circuit (Figure 27.1). What happens to the rate of flow of balls at point P in the circuit when the clamp squashes the pipe? What happens to the rate of flow at Q?

Wherever the pipe is squashed, the current in the whole circuit is reduced. If you squash the pipe at P, it reduces the flow at Q as well. Compare this with an electrical circuit.

Dimming a light bulb, measuring current all the way round

- Set up the first circuit (Figure 27.2). Note the brightness of the lamp.
- Then set up the next circuit with a resistor.
- Now use a variable resistor. Adjust it and note the effect.
- Put ammeters in the wires and measure the current all the way round.
- Then try putting the resistor on the other side of the lamp.

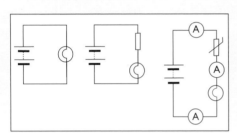

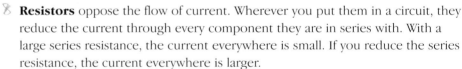

Figure 27.2   Measuring current in series circuits

Controlling current

Resistors oppose the flow of current. Wherever you put them in a circuit, they reduce the current through every component they are in series with. With a large series resistance, the current everywhere is small. If you reduce the series resistance, the current everywhere is larger.

You can put extra resistance into an electrical circuit simply by making part of the circuit thinner. Or you can include a much longer wire. You can also add extra resistance by putting in a piece of material through which electrons find it hard to move, or in which there are very few charge carriers that can move.

Figure 27.3   A thermistor and a light-dependent resistor

Electrical sensors

An electrical sensor feeds information into a circuit by allowing a physical quantity outside the circuit to control current flow. Many electrical sensors make use of a changing resistance. One type of light sensor, a **light-dependent resistor** (LDR), changes resistance with the level of illumination. A **thermistor** changes resistance with temperature. Both are shown in Figure 27.3.

Thermistor and LDR

- Use a thermistor and a light-emitting diode to make a crude thermometer using the circuit shown in Figure 27.4.
- Then use a light-dependent resistor in place of the thermistor to make a crude light meter.
- Modify the circuits with a buzzer to make a temperature alarm or a light alarm that will switch a buzzer on if the temperature gets high or if the light gets bright.
- Now try making a circuit that will start a motor when the LDR is illuminated.

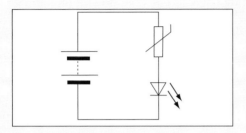

Figure 27.4   A crude thermometer

Series and parallel

So far you have looked at current flowing in a series circuit. But components can be connected in parallel, as well as in series–parallel combinations. Figures 27.5 to 27.7 show all these possibilities.

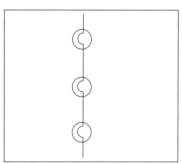

Figure 27.5   Components connected in series

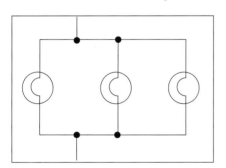

Figure 27.6   Components connected in parallel

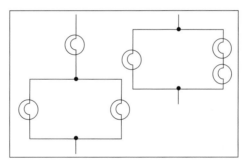

Figure 27.7   Series–parallel arrangements

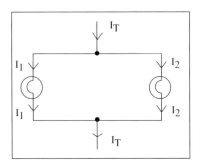

Figure 27.9 Current in a parallel circuit, $I_T = I_1 + I_2$

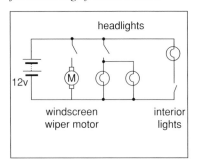

Figure 27.10 The flow leaving by route 3 is equal to the sum of the flows arriving by routes 1 and 2

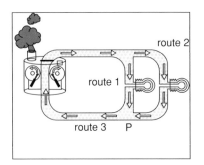

Figure 27.11 Car wiring uses parallel circuits

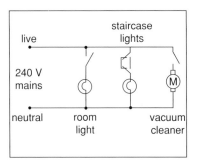

Figure 27.12 House wiring also uses parallel circuits

Currents in parallel circuits

Figure 27.9 is a **parallel** circuit. The current I_T from the cell splits at the junction. Part of it, I_1, goes through the lamp on the left; the rest, I_2, goes through the lamp on the right. The sum of these two currents I_1 and I_2 is I_T. If the lamps are identical then the two currents will be identical. But components which are in parallel are often different, so the current through them will be different too.

The mechanical circuit in Figure 27.10 gives an idea of what is going on. Some of the balls can take route 1, others take route 2. At point P, the number of balls arriving via route 1 and route 2 is equal to the number leaving by route 3.

Kirchhoff's first law

If you examine a circuit in which a steady current is flowing you find that, at any junction in a circuit, the amount of charge entering is equal to the amount of charge that leaves. Similarly, the rate at which charge flows in to any point is equal to the rate at which charge flows out of the point. The current entering a point is equal to the current leaving that point. This is called **Kirchhoff's first law**:

> The sum of the currents entering a point is equal to the sum of the currents leaving that point.

Kirchhoff's first law is a consequence of the fact that charge is conserved. It can be regarded as a law of conservation of charge. It states that no charge is lost in a circuit or at any junction in a circuit.

Measuring current in parallel circuits

- Set up the circuits in Figure 27.8 and use an ammeter to measure the current through every accessible wire.
- When you have done one or two measurements on each circuit, predict what the rest of your readings will be before you take the measurements.

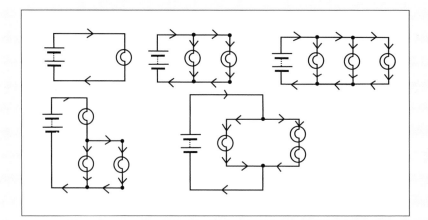

Figure 27.8 Measuring current in parallel circuits

Uses of parallel circuits

When power supplies are connected to components in parallel, the current through each branch of the parallel circuit depends mostly on the resistance of the branch itself, and is independent of what goes on in other branches. Provided that the supply is powerful enough to supply current to all the components that are in parallel, the current through one branch does not affect the current through the others. Car wiring (Figure 27.11), house wiring (Figure 27.12), the wiring of different modules in a piece of electronic equipment, and any other wiring where each part needs to be independent of the other part, all use parallel wiring.

Controlling a small current with a large current

An LDR will not pass enough current to run a motor. If you want to make a light-controlled motor, you need a device that will enable a sensor like an LDR, which can control only a small current, to control a larger current. The reed relay (Figure 27.13) uses an electromagnet to control a switch. When a current flows through the electromagnet coil, the switch contacts are magnetised and pull themselves together. The current needed to pull the contacts together is much less than the current that can flow through the contacts. The reed relay can thus control a large current with a small current.

The controlling current and the controlled current flow in two loops that have some parts in common and some separate. Where they separate, the components through which they each pass are in parallel.

The transistor

A transistor can also control a large current with a small current. In some ways it is an electronic relay. Figure 27.14 shows a transistor used to help an LDR control a motor.

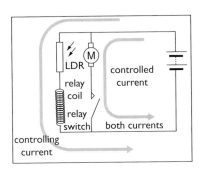

Figure 27.13   Reed relay control

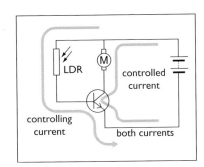

Figure 27.14   Transistor control

Cells and voltage

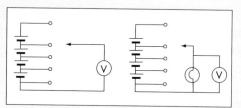

- Set up the circuits shown in Figure 28.1.
- Connect the voltmeter across one cell and note the reading.
- Then measure across two, three and four cells.
- Now observe what happens when you connect a lamp to increasing numbers of cells.

Figure 28.1   What is the effect of the number of cells?

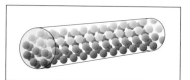

Figure 28.2   With no forces, the balls remain stationary

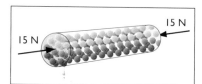

Figure 28.3   With equal forces, the balls also remain stationary

Figure 28.4   When the forces on the balls are unequal, the balls accelerate

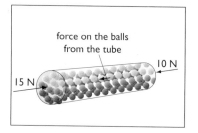

Figure 28.5   When the resistance from the tube equals the external force difference, the balls go at constant speed

Pushing harder

When you connect cells together in series, the voltmeter indicates a larger voltage. When you increase the number of cells in series to a lamp, the lamp glows brighter, showing that the current is greater. You know that if the current increases then the charge is flowing faster. If the charge is flowing faster through the same resistance, it is being pushed harder, and the higher voltage indicates that.

Creating a flow

Think about a pipe full of balls (Figure 28.2). With no force acting on them, the balls would not accelerate. If they were stationary, they would not start moving.

On the other hand, if there were equal forces at both ends of the pipe (Figure 28.3), the net force would be zero, and the balls would still not accelerate. If stationary, they would still not start to move.

The balls start moving when the force pushing the balls in one direction is greater than the force pushing them in the other direction (Figure 28.4). It is the force difference applied across the tube that starts the balls going.

But there is friction inside the tube, which resists the flow of balls. The balls reach a steady speed when the force difference across the tube is equal to the resistance caused by friction within the tube (Figure 28.5).

The same situation arises with electrons in a wire. When a steady current flows, the average drift speed of the charge carriers is constant. This means that the average resultant force on the carriers is zero. The power supply pushes the electrons in the direction that they are going, and the circuit resistances hinder the flow. So the resultant force on the electrons is zero.

Voltage difference

In a mechanical circuit, force difference drives the flow. In electrical circuits, voltage difference drives current through a component. If the voltage across a component increases, it pushes the charge carriers harder. They will move faster and the current will increase.

Another name for voltage is potential; it is common to talk about the potential difference (p.d.) across a component. Sometimes this is referred to as the voltage across a component. You connect a voltmeter *across* a component to measure the voltage difference between its ends.

If the voltages at the ends of a component are the same, there is no voltage across the component. So no current will flow. This is like connecting both ends of a component to the same terminal of a battery (Figure 28.6).

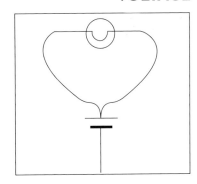

Figure 28.6   If both leads from the lamp are connected to the same terminal, it does not light

Measuring voltage

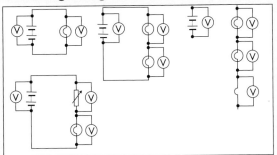

Figure 28.7   Measuring voltage in series circuits

- Measure the voltages across the components in the circuits shown in Figure 28.7.
- When you have taken one or two measurements, predict what the remaining measurements will be before taking them.
- Label your diagrams with the voltages across each component.

Pushing and resisting

If, as you go round a circuit, you keep the terminals of your voltmeter the same way round, you find that for some components the reading is positive; for the rest the reading is negative.

As you move the voltmeter clockwise round the circuit of Figure 28.8, keeping its negative terminal anticlockwise of the positive terminal, the meter goes positive for those components which are helping charge move (in this case the cells) and negative for those which are resisting. If you go right round any series circuit, the sum of the voltages across the components pushing is equal to the sum of the voltages across the components resisting.

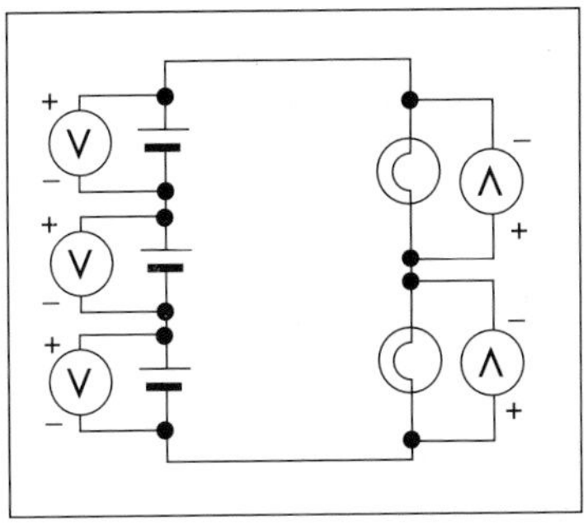

Electrical and water currents

The flow of balls through a pipe is something like the flow of a current of water through a pipe. Indeed the analogy is very close if you think of water as made up of many ball-like atoms. It is *pressure difference* that drives water flow, and this is a better analogy for voltage difference than the model with force difference. Pressure, like voltage, is a scalar quantity, whereas force is a vector. Voltage or pressure differences drive electrical or water currents. Electrical or pipe resistances oppose the flow. In both situations, the rate of flow is the current.

Figure 28.8   Keeping the voltmeter the same way round shows which components are helping and which are hindering

Electrical power and energy calculations

Electromotive forces–energy givers

Some components in an electrical circuit push the charge carriers in the direction the carriers move. They are working on the charge and so give energy to the circuit. Components like cells and generators do work on the charge. Voltages across these components are called **electromotive forces** (e.m.f.s), because they apply forces that make the charge move.

Potential differences–energy takers

The other components in the circuit, the wires, the lamps, the resistors, etc, apply forces in the opposite direction to the direction the charge is moving. The charge does work on them, transferring energy to them. The voltages across them are called **potential differences** (p.d.s). As you would expect, the total amount of energy given to a circuit by the e.m.f.'s is equal to the total amount of energy taken by the p.d.s. Around a loop in a series circuit, the e.m.f.s = the p.d.s (Figure 29.1). You might like to reread the section 'Pushing and resisting' in Chapter 28 and compare it with this statement. (The term potential difference is mostly used for energy takers, but sometimes used for energy givers as well. It does, however, help to keep the ideas separate if you use the different terms.)

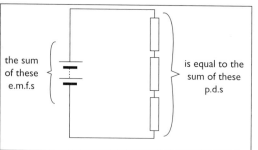

Figure 29.1   The e.m.f.s = the p.d.s

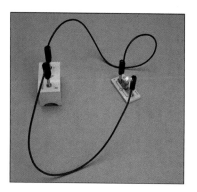

Figure 29.2   A cell working on a lamp

Calculating work done

Voltage can be used to calculate the work done pushing the charge carriers round a circuit or through a component. The **voltage** between two points is the work done per coulomb travelling between the two points. That is

voltage = work/charge

$$V = W/Q$$

So the unit of voltage, the volt, is the same as the units of work/charge, i.e. joule/coulomb:

$$1\ V = 1\ J\ C^{-1}$$

If the voltage across the cell in Figure 29.2 is 1.5 V, the cell gives 1.5 joules per coulomb that travels between the terminals. There is, of course, a voltage of 1.5 V across the lamp as well. So 1.5 J of work is done on the lamp every time a coulomb goes through the lamp.

If a 230 V power supply is connected to a motor, then the work done when 8 coulombs flow can be calculated by:

$$\text{work} = \text{voltage} \times \text{charge} = 230\ J\ C^{-1} \times 8\ C = 1840\ J$$

So 1840 joules of energy is transferred from the power supply to the motor when 8 coulombs flow.

Measuring work and power

- Connect a power supply to a lamp. Measure the voltage across the lamp and the current through the lamp.
- Calculate how much charge passes through the lamp in one minute. Then calculate the work done in that time.
- Calculate the charge that flows in one second and the work done in a second.

Calculating power

Power is the work done per second. Since

work = voltage × charge

then

power = work/time = voltage × charge/time

power = voltage × current

$P = VI$

You can use this equation to define the voltage between two points as the power transferred to the circuit between those points per amp.

The unit of power is, of course, the joule per second or watt. You can see that

$$\frac{\text{joule}}{\text{second}} = \frac{\text{joule}}{\text{coulomb}} \times \frac{\text{coulomb}}{\text{second}}$$

Voltage across components in series

When components are in series (Figure 29.3), the total voltage across all the components is equal to the sum of the voltages across each individual component.

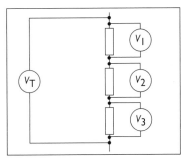

Figure 29.3   Voltage across components in series, $V_T = V_1 + V_2 + V_3$

Measuring voltage in parallel circuits

- Set up the circuits in Figure 30.1 and measure the voltages across each component.
- Then try other circuits.
- What rules can you find for the voltages across components that are in parallel?

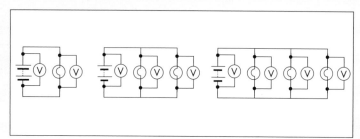

Figure 30.1   Measuring voltage in parallel circuits

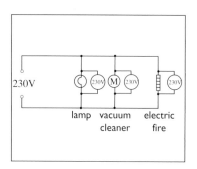

Figure 30.2   Components connected to the mains supply are in parallel. They have the same voltage across them

Voltage across components in parallel

When components are in parallel, the voltage across each component is the same. In Chapter 27 you learned that the currents in a parallel circuit can be more or less independent of each other, which is why components are connected in parallel when connected to the mains supply or to a car battery. Now you can see that components connected in parallel have the same voltage across them. A 230 V lamp can be connected in parallel with a 230 V vacuum cleaner and a 230 V electric fire, all to a 230 V supply, and they all have the same supply voltage.

Flowing streams

Sometimes it is useful to think of an electric current as being rather like a water current.

Imagine a mountain with two streams flowing down it (Figure 30.3). The streams flow because the mountain is sloping. The water flows from high parts to lower parts.

Is it height that causes a stream to flow? No, it is not. Water high up on mountains is often in still pools. Even though it is high, it is not flowing. On the other hand you find flowing streams in low valleys. Water does not need to be high in order to flow.

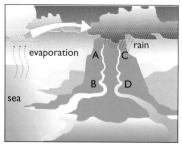

Figure 30.3   A water circuit

What you need to make water flow is a height difference and a suitable pathway. Water flows from one place to another if the first place is high and the second place is low. On the two streams, points A, B, C and D are marked. A and C are at the same height; B and D are at the same height. If you dug a channel from A to C (Figure 30.4) there would be no height difference and no flow. The same would happen if you dug a channel from B to D. But if you dug a channel from A to D (Figure 30.5) then there would be a height difference and the water would flow. The rate of flow (the current) would depend on the height difference and the size of the channel. A short fat channel would have a low resistance to water flow and the current would be relatively high. The current in a long thin channel would be relatively small.

In the water circuit, rain provides the water for the streams. As the streams flow in to the valleys, the sun causes evaporation, which supplies the clouds. This completes the water circuit. In the steady state, the amount of water flowing down the mountain is equal to the amount being taken up by evaporation.

Electrical height

In the water cycle, the sun provides the power source to pump the water around and the flow is a water current. In an electrical circuit, a battery or a generator provides the power source to pump the charge around. The flow of charge is a current. In both circuits, the current is larger if the paths are short and fat.

Look at the two 'electrical streams' in Figure 30.6. The battery pushes charge 'uphill' to the top of the circuit and the charge flows 'downhill' through the two chains of resistors. If all the resistors are identical, you can see that point A is at the same electrical height as point C. There is no electrical height difference between points A and C. It does not matter what wires, resistors or meters you connect between points A and C, no current will flow between these two points. Similarly, there is no electrical height difference between points B and D, and no current will flow in a wire that connects them.

But there *is* an electrical height difference between points A and D; a current will flow in any wire you connect between them. You know that it is voltage difference that drives a current. Voltage (or potential) is the electrical equivalent of height.

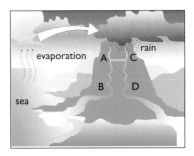

Figure 30.4 There is no flow through this channel from A to C, because there is no height difference

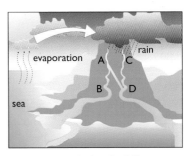

Figure 30.5 The height difference between A and D causes the flow through the channel

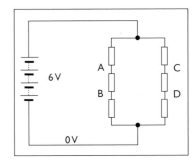

Figure 30.6 The battery pushes charge through the electrical streams AB and CD

Kirchhoff's second law

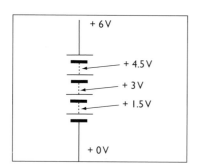

Figure 31.1 Voltages at different points in a battery

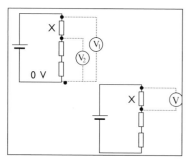

Figure 31.2 Two ways of measuring the voltage across a component X: (a) either measure the voltage at each end of X and subtract them, $V_X = V_1 - V_2$; or (b) measure the voltage across X directly, $V_X = V$

Voltage at a point

You can mark heights on a map to show how much higher, or lower, a point is relative to some reference level (usually sea level). Similarly, if you want to mark voltages on a circuit, you need to choose some point as a zero of voltage. In experiments with electrostatics you may use the earth on which you are standing as the zero of potential. Electrical engineers commonly choose a reference point for all their voltage measurements which they label 0 V. This point is usually at the bottom of a circuit, but sometimes it is in the middle. The **voltage at a point** in the circuit is the voltage difference between zero and that point. Figure 31.1 shows a battery with the voltages at different points labelled.

If you look back to Figure 30.6, you see that the bottom line is labelled 0 V. That is the zero of voltage for that circuit. The battery is a 6 V battery. That means that the top line of the circuit has a voltage of +6 V. If the resistors are all identical, you can calculate that the voltage of points A and C is +4 V and the voltage of points B and D is +2 V.

Voltage across a component

The **voltage across a component** is simply the difference in voltage between the two ends. You can use a voltmeter to measure the voltage at each end relative to 0 V and then subtract the readings, or you can simply connect a voltmeter across the two points to measure the voltage difference directly (Figure 31.2).

If you look back again to Figure 30.6, you can work out that the voltage difference between A and B (the voltage across the middle resistor) is 2 V. Similarly, the voltage across the bottom left or bottom right resistor is 2 V.

Producing a voltage–position graph

- For each circuit in Figure 31.3, connect the 0 V terminal of a digital voltmeter to the part of the circuit marked 0 V.
- Use the other lead to measure the voltage at point A.
- Then predict what the voltages might be at points B to E, before measuring them.

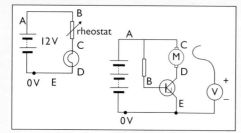

Figure 31.3 Circuits for measurement of voltage at different positions

Voltage–position graph

Figure 31.4 shows a series circuit with a graph of potential plotted against position for that circuit. Notice how the voltage increases through the e.m.f.s and decreases through the p.d.s. Notice also the small voltages across the connecting wires that drive the current through them.

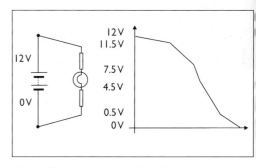

Figure 31.4   A series circuit and its voltage–position graph

Kirchhoff's second law

Think what happens if you take a walk up a hill and back down again, a closed loop. When you arrive back at your starting point, you are back at the same height you were at in the beginning. For the whole loop, the amount of height gained is equal to the amount of height lost.

Kirchhoff's second law states the equivalent for an electrical circuit. It states that, around a closed loop in a circuit, the gain in voltage is equal to the loss in voltage. In other words, you arrive back at the same electrical height that you started from. The gains in voltage are caused by the e.m.f.s, the drops are caused by the p.d.s. **Kirchhoff's second law** states that:

> Around any closed loop, the sum of the e.m.f.s is equal to the sum of the p.d.s.

Kirchhoff II is a statement about voltage. And since voltage is a measure of the work done, or energy transferred, per unit charge, this means that Kirchhoff II is also a statement about energy. It states that the total amount of energy gained by a coulomb going round a complete circuit is equal to the total amount of energy lost. In this way you can regard Kirchhoff II as one version of the law of conservation of energy.

Figure 31.5 shows two circuit diagrams showing typical voltages at various points. Look at the diagrams. Do they make sense? Work out which way currents would flow if wires were connected between different points in the circuit.

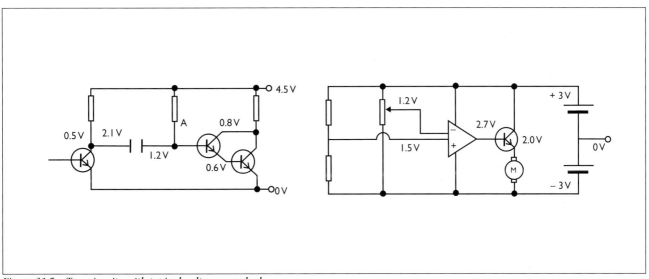

Figure 31.5   Two circuits with typical voltages marked

What is resistance?

All components need a voltage to push current through them. When the resistance is high you need a large voltage for a given current. When the resistance is low you need a small voltage. The **resistance** indicates the voltage you need for each amp of current:

$$resistance = voltage/current$$

$$R = V/I$$

The unit of resistance is the volt per amp, which is called the ohm (Ω).

Measuring the resistance of a component

- Use a voltmeter and ammeter to measure the resistances of a range of components (Figure 32.1).
- Then connect two or more of them in series and investigate how the total resistance depends on the individual resistances.
- Then connect your components in parallel pairs and investigate how the total resistance depends on the individual resistances.

Figure 32.1 Finding the resistance of a component by measuring the voltage across it and the current through it

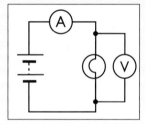

Figure 32.2 You can use a digital ohmmeter to measure resistance directly

Resistors in series

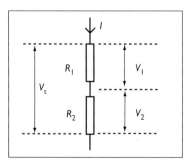

Figure 32.3 Resistors in series

The total resistance of a number of components in series is simply the sum of the individual resistances.

Resistances R_1 and R_2 are connected in series with a current I flowing through them (Figure 32.3). The voltage across the whole, V_t, is the sum of the individual voltages across each resistor:

$$V_t = V_1 + V_2$$

The equivalent resistance, R_t, is defined by

$$V_t = IR_t$$

But $V_1 = IR_1$ and $V_2 = IR_2$. Therefore

$$IR_t = IR_1 + IR_2$$

$$R_t = R_1 + R_2$$

Resistors in parallel

Each extra resistor in parallel provides an additional path for current to go through, and so allows more current for a given voltage. The resistance of a number of resistors in parallel is *less* than the smallest of the individual resistances.

The voltage across the resistors in Figure 32.4 is V. The total current I_t flowing into and out of the parallel combination is the sum of the currents I_1 and I_2 through the individual resistors:

$$I_t = I_1 + I_2$$

The equivalent resistance, R_t, is defined by

$$R_t = V/I_t$$

Therefore $I_t = V/R_t$. Similarly $I_1 = V/R_1$ and $I_2 = V/R_2$. Since $I_t = I_1 + I_2$,

$$\frac{V}{R_t} = \frac{V}{R_1} + \frac{V}{R_2}$$

$$\frac{1}{R_t} = \frac{1}{R_1} + \frac{1}{R_2}$$

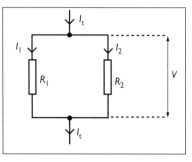

Figure 32.4   Resistors in parallel

For a resistance of 220 Ω in parallel with a resistance of 470 Ω,

$$1/R_t = 1/R_1 + 1/R_2$$

$$1/R_t = 1/220 + 1/470$$

$$1/R_t = 6.67 \times 10^{-3}\ \Omega^{-1}$$

$$R_t = 150\ \Omega$$

Calculating power from current through resistance

When a current flows through a resistor, work is done on that resistor. You can calculate the power, the rate of working, directly from the current and resistance.

When a resistor is connected to a voltage V, power $= VI$
But the voltage across the resistor, $V = IR$. So

$$\text{power} = (IR) \times I = I^2R$$

If a resistance of 6.8 kΩ has a current of 2.2 mA flowing through it,

$$\text{power} = I^2R = (2.2 \times 10^{-3}\ \text{A})^2 \times 6.8 \times 10^3\ \Omega = 0.033\ \text{W} = 33\ \text{mW}$$

When a current flows through a resistor, we sometimes say that the power is **dissipated**. This means scattered. The internal energy of the resistor has increased, and this random kinetic and potential energy gradually spreads to the surroundings. You can read more about energy dissipation in the text for Module 3.

Resistivity

What affects the resistance of a wire?

- Use an ohmmeter to measure the resistance of different lengths of a constant thickness of thin nichrome wire.
- Plot a graph to determine the relationship between resistance and length.
- Then measure the resistance of equal lengths of a range of thicknesses. Use a micrometer to measure their diameters and calculate their cross-sectional areas.
- Plot a graph to determine the relationship between resistance and cross-sectional area.
- Repeat with wires made from different metals.

Resistivity

The resistance of a wire depends on several factors. A long wire has a larger resistance than a short wire. A fat wire has a lower resistance than a thin wire. Resistance is proportional to length and inversely proportional to cross-sectional area; and it depends on a property of the material called **resistivity**. So

$$\text{resistance} = \text{resistivity} \times \frac{\text{length}}{\text{area}}$$

$$R = \rho l / A$$

Resistivity, ρ, is a property of the material (whereas resistance is a property of a component). Resistivity is a measure of how the material opposes the current through it. Metals have a low resistivity; insulators have a high resistivity. Semiconductors, as their name implies, are somewhere in the middle. Table 32.1 lists typical values of resistivity.

For example, the resistance of 100 m of copper wire, cross-sectional area 1.5 mm², is

$$\frac{R = \rho l}{A} = \frac{1.72 \times 10^{-8}\ \Omega\text{m} \times 100\ \text{m}}{1.5 \times 10^{-6}\ \text{m}^2} = 1.15\ \Omega$$

Table 32.1 *The resistivities of various materials*

Material	Resistivity/Ωm
metals	
copper	1.7×10^{-8}
iron	10×10^{-8}
semiconductors	
graphite	10^{-5} (very variable)
silicon	10^{5}
insulators	
paraffin wax	10^{15}
porcelain	10^{20}

Electrons drifting

The evidence for what goes on inside a conducting material is indirect. Physicists make a model for conduction which fits the evidence. The outer electrons of the atoms in a metal are free from their parent atom, leaving behind an ion vibrating about a fixed position. At normal temperatures, with no current flowing, electrons in a wire hurtle around continuously (Figure 33.1). They keep colliding with the metal ions, but on balance no energy is transferred from electrons to the ions. Since the electrons move randomly, there is no net movement of charge in any direction.

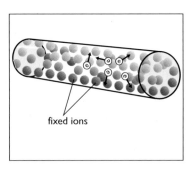

fixed ions

Figure 33.1 Electrons hurtle about in a wire

When a power supply is connected across a wire, it causes electrons to accelerate from negative to positive. The electrons then collide with the fixed ions and move off in a random direction and are then accelerated again by the power supply (Figure 33.2). The electrons are continuously gaining energy from the supply and giving it to the ions when they collide. The ions gain energy and the metal gets hotter.

The constant acceleration and collision result in a steady, slow drift along the conductor, superimposed on top of the huge random velocities. This tiny drift speed of a fraction of a millimetre per second is almost unobservable on top of the random velocity of hundreds of metres per second. But it is responsible for all the electrical effects you observe.

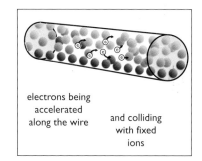

Figure 33.2   Electrons accelerate and then collide when a power supply is connected across the wire

Change of resistance of a metal

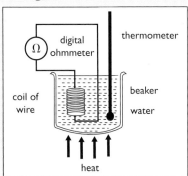

- Set up the apparatus shown in Figure 33.3.
- Measure the resistance of a coil of 10 m of thin insulated copper wire over a range of temperatures.
- Plot a graph of resistance against temperature.

Figure 33.3   The resistance of a metal wire at constant temperature

Change of carrier speed with temperature

For all materials the fixed ions have larger vibrations at higher temperatures, and increased vibrations impede further the movement of electrons through the metal, tending to reduce the drift speed of the carriers. For pure metals this is the dominant effect, and it means that the resistance of a metal increases with temperature. In other materials this effect is present, though it is not always the most important effect.

Change of resistance of thermistor and light-dependent resistor

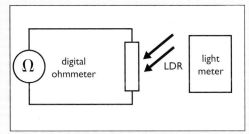

- Measure the resistance of a negative-temperature-coefficient thermistor over a range of temperatures. Plot a graph of resistance against temperature.
- Measure the resistance of a light-dependent resistor for a range of values of illumination (Figure 33.4). Plot a graph of resistance against light intensity measured with a light meter.
- Repeat with lights of different colour.

Figure 33.4   The resistance of an LDR

Changes in carrier density

In **metals**, the carrier density n is high and does not change with temperature. In **semiconductors**, the carrier density is much smaller but increases strongly with temperature. Therefore, unless some other effect intervenes, the resistivity of a semiconductor decreases with temperature. Thermistors and light-dependent resistors are made of semiconductor materials.

Change of resistance and the equation $I = nAqv$

In metals, currents involve large numbers of charge carriers moving very slowly. When the temperature increases, the drift speed v decreases while the charge-carrier density n is constant. So, while the area A and carrier charge q are constant, the current I in a metallic conductor decreases with temperature because v decreases while n stays the same.

In semiconductors, currents are produced by many fewer carriers moving comparatively quickly. As with metals, the drift speed of the carriers tends to decrease with increasing temperature, but the carrier density increases enormously at higher temperatures. So, while the area A and carrier charge q are constant, the current I in a semiconductor increases with temperature because, though v decreases a little with temperature, n increases enormously.

Negative-temperature-coefficient (NTC) thermistors behave like this. There is a second type of thermistor called positive-temperature-coefficient (PTC). In these, n changes little with temperature, but v decreases significantly, increasing the resistance.

For insulators, n is very small indeed at normal temperatures, but increases for all insulators if the temperature is raised sufficiently for the atomic structure to break down into charged particles. Glass (Figures 33.5) is an example.

For some cleverly constructed materials, the increase in n compensates for the decrease in v, so the resistivity stays the same. The carbon used in commercial resistors is tailored to have very little change in resistivity with temperature, as is constantan, an alloy used for making precision resistors.

Light-dependent resistors also make use of changing n. When they are illuminated, photons in the incident radiation free charge carriers, so they conduct much better and their resistance falls.

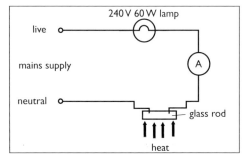

Figure 33.5   When the glass conducts, the current is limited by the lamp and measured by the ammeter

The potential divider

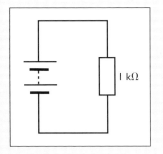

Figure 34.1   Measure the voltage across one 1 kΩ resistor

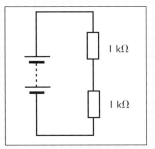

Figure 34.2   Measure the voltage across two 1 kΩ resistors in series

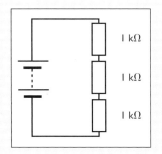

Figure 34.3   Measure the voltage across three 1 kΩ resistors in series

Chains of resistors

Experiments with a series of identical resistors show that the voltage across each of them is the same and adds up to the voltage across the whole chain (Figures 34.4 and 34.5). With a series of resistors, you can divide a voltage into any fraction.

Flowing downhill

Think back to the height analogy of an electrical circuit. Current is flowing down a resistance chain rather like water flowing down a hillside (Figure 34.6). If the stream flows along a uniform channel down a smooth slope, the midpoint B will be half-way down the hill. The height difference BC is half the height difference AC. In the electrical circuit, the voltage difference BC is half of the voltage difference AC.

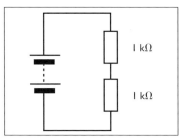

Figure 34.4   If the resistors are identical, then the voltages across each are the same. The voltage across each is half of the whole

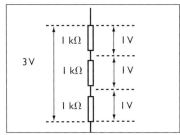

Figure 34.5   With three identical resistors in series, the voltage across each is one-third of the whole

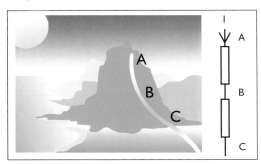

Figure 34.6   Current flows through a chain of resistors like water through a channel

The voltages across different resistors

- Connect a 1 kΩ and a 2 kΩ resistor across the power supply and measure the voltage across each.
- Predict your results before measuring.

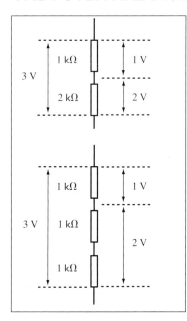

Figure 34.7   The 2 kΩ resistor is like two 1 kΩ resistors in series

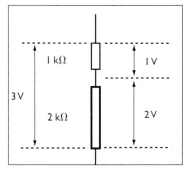

Figure 34.8   Most of the voltage is across the largest resistor

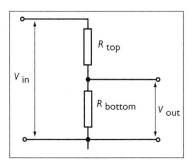

Figure 34.9   The potential divider

Chains of different resistors

If the two resistors in series are different, there are different voltages across them. For instance, if the bottom resistor is twice the resistance of the top resistor (Figure 34.7), it behaves like two resistors connected in series and there is twice as much voltage across it.

Experiments with a range of resistances show that the ratio of the voltages across the resistors is equal to the ratio of the resistances.

In circuit diagrams resistors have standard symbols, but it helps understanding to think of drawing the resistors with length proportional to resistance. In Figure 34.8 the voltage across the top resistance is smaller than the voltage across the bottom one.

Circuits like these are voltage dividers, but they are usually called **potential dividers**. They divide the voltage or p.d. from a source in proportion to their resistances.

Calculating the output of a potential divider

Think of a potential divider (Figure 34.9) as having an input connected to a power supply (V_{in}) and an output (V_{out}). The input voltage to the circuit is the voltage across both resistors. The output voltage is the voltage across the bottom resistor. Provided that no current is drawn from the output, the same current I flows through both resistors.

$$I = \frac{V_{out}}{R_{bottom}} = \frac{V_{in}}{R_{top} + R_{bottom}}$$

$$\therefore \quad V_{out} = V_{in} \frac{R_{bottom}}{R_{top} + R_{bottom}}$$

For example, if the top resistance is 1.2 kΩ and the bottom resistance 720 Ω, then the output, when connected to an input of 12 V, is

$$V_{out} = V_{in} \frac{R_{bottom}}{(R_{top} + R_{bottom})} = 12 \times \frac{720\Omega}{1200\Omega + 720\Omega} = 4.5 \text{ V}$$

Light- and temperature-sensitive potential dividers

- Set up the circuit shown in Figure 34.10.
- Use a voltmeter to find out how V_{out} depends on the level of illumination.
- Then exchange the position of the LDR and the resistance and find how the circuit behaves differently.
- Repeat the exercise using a thermistor instead of an LDR and investigate how the circuit behaviour depends on temperature.

Figure 34.10 Light-sensitive potential divider

Using an LDR or a thermistor to control voltage

You can use a light-dependent resistor with another fixed resistor to produce a potential divider that is sensitive to light (Figure 34.11). When the LDR is in the dark, its resistance is high and the voltage across it is relatively large. When the LDR is in the light, its resistance is small and the voltage across it is relatively small (Figure 34.12).

The voltage across the fixed resistor in this circuit changes when the resistance of the LDR changes. This is not because the fixed resistor itself has changed, but because the changes in the resistance of the LDR change the current in the circuit.

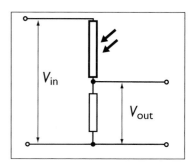

Figure 34.11 When the LDR is dark, its resistance is high

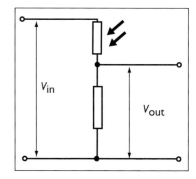

Figure 34.12 When the LDR is in the light, its resistance is low

V-I Characteristics

Providing a variable voltage

- Set up the circuits shown in Figures 35.1 and 35.2.
- Use your theory of the potential divider to predict the voltages across the lamps in these two circuits.
- Why do they behave as they do?

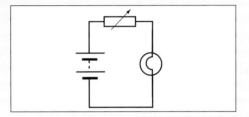

Figure 35.1   Controlling a lamp with a rheostat

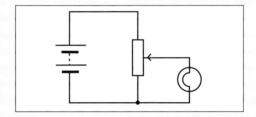

Figure 35.2   Controlling a lamp with a potentiometer

Rheostats

A variable resistance in series with a component is often called a **rheostat**. It controls the current through the component. A rheostat has a maximum resistance and so some current will still flow through it even at this setting. So it cannot reduce and control the current down to zero.

Potentiometers

A **potentiometer** is a variable potential divider. A sliding contact can connect anywhere from one end to the other of a long resistor chain and so can take any fraction of the whole voltage. So it can vary the voltage across a component, and therefore the current through it, from maximum down to zero (Figure 35.3).

Though linear (straight) potentiometers are available, most potentiometers are circular (Figure 35.4).

Loading potentiometers

When a resistance is connected to the output of the potential divider, it is connected in parallel with the bottom resistor of the potential divider. The combined resistance at the bottom of the potential divider is less and so this lowers the output voltage of the potential divider. This is called loading the potential divider (Figure 35.5).

Digital voltmeters are electronic voltmeters. A battery inside them supplies the operating current. These voltmeters have high resistance and they draw very little current from the circuit to which they are connected. The load they present to the potential divider is usually negligible and they usually hardly affect the voltage they are measuring.

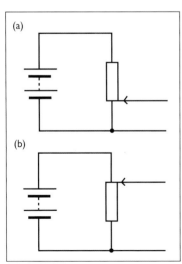

Figure 35.3   The output of a potentiometer can vary from (a) low to (b) maximum

Analogue voltmeters, unless they are electronic ones, need to draw enough current from the circuit to which they are connected to move the mechanical pointer. Even though their resistance is high, the small current they draw can significantly change the voltage they measure if you connect them to a potential divider made of high resistances.

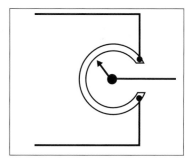

Figure 35.4 Volume controls for radios and amplifiers use circular potentiometers. You rotate a shaft to move the contact

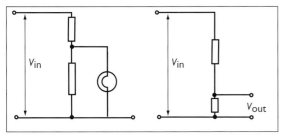

Figure 35.5 The lamp in parallel with the lower resistance reduces the total resistance at the bottom

Voltage–current characteristics

The bigger the voltage across a component, the harder the charge is pushed, so the larger the current. But the way that the current increases with potential difference varies from component to component. Each component has **V–I characteristics** which show how current varies with voltage.

How does current vary with voltage?

- The simplest variable voltage supply is a battery pack (Figure 35.6). This gives a supply that can be varied in steps of about 1.5 V. You can measure the current for each different voltage.
- You can get a continuously variable voltage by using a potentiometer (Figure 35.7) to control the voltage between zero and maximum.
- For a number of different components, measure the current for a range of voltages.
- Reverse the component to push current in the opposite direction and repeat your readings.
- Draw a graph of current against voltage, including both positive and negative currents and voltages, to show the behaviour of the components.
- For each component, calculate the resistance for a number of values of voltage. Plot a graph of resistance against voltage.

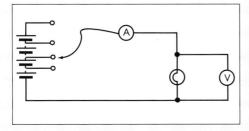

Figure 35.6 Separate cells can be used to provide a variable voltage

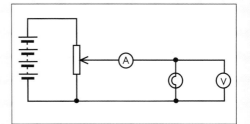

Figure 35.7 A potentiometer connected to a battery pack can also be used to provide a variable voltage

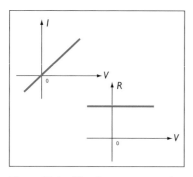

Figure 35.8 The characteristics of a resistor

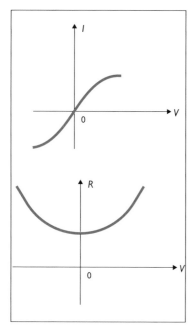

Figure 35.9 The resistance of this lamp increases at higher voltages and currents, because it gets hotter

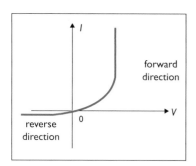

Figure 35.10 This semiconductor diode allows current to flow only in the forward direction

Ohm's law

All components resist the flow of current in some way or other. You know that the resistance is given by

$$R = V/I$$

For some components, the resistance is constant. So the current through a component is proportional to the voltage across it. This is called **Ohm's law**. Ohm's law applies to many resistors (Figure 35.8) and to many metals at constant temperature. Such components are **ohmic**.

Tungsten filament lamp

For a tungsten filament lamp, the current increases when the voltage increases, but the curve of the graph (Figure 35.9) shows that doubling the voltage produces less than double the current. This is because the filament gets hotter as the current increases and the resistance of the filament increases as it gets hotter.

With care, you can crack the glass of a lamp and measure the characteristics with the filament immersed in water. The filament behaves ohmically and its resistance stays constant, because the temperature stays constant.

Semiconductor diode

The **diode** allows current to flow freely in one direction only (Figure 35.10). This is called the **forward direction**. The current increases rapidly as soon as the forward voltage is greater than about 0.5 V. In the **reverse direction**, very little current flows.

The LED has characteristics that are very similar to an ordinary semiconductor diode, but it needs a greater forward voltage to get the current flowing through it and emits light when it conducts.

Thermistor

Figure 35.11 shows the characteristics of a thermistor with a negative temperature coefficient, which means that its resistance decreases with temperature. It conducts better as the voltage and current get larger; when the voltage doubles, the current more than doubles. The thermistor gets hotter as voltage and current increase, because more power is dissipated in it. The higher temperature frees more charge carriers, and reduces the resistance.

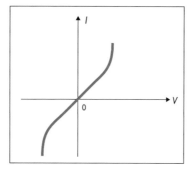

Figure 35.11 A negative-temperature-coefficient thermistor conducts better when V and I become large

Symmetry

Most electrical components behave symmetrically so that the variation of *I* with *V* is the same whichever way round the voltage is connected. Other components, like diodes, are asymmetrical; they behave differently if you reverse the voltage.

Different ways of measuring voltage and current

- Set up the circuits in Figures 35.12 and 35.13.
- Use these two different circuits to measure the voltage across, and the current through, the 10 kΩ resistor.
- Take the readings very carefully indeed and compare them.

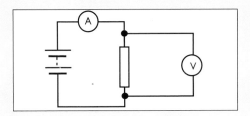

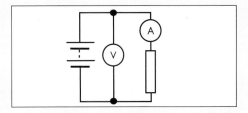

Figure 35.12   Circuit 1 for measuring voltage and current

Figure 35.13   Circuit 2 for measuring voltage and current

Errors caused by voltmeters and ammeters

The two arrangements of the meters for measuring *V–I* characteristics (Figures 35.12 and 35.13) both introduce small errors in measurement.

As you read in Chapter 34, even though the resistance of voltmeters is high, they draw a tiny current when you connect them to a voltage. In Figure 35.12, the voltmeter reads correctly, but the ammeter measures the current through the resistor and the voltmeter. So there is a small error since you assume that the ammeter reading is the current through the resistor alone.

Ammeters have a small but significant resistance; when current flows through them, there is a voltage across them. In Figure 35.12, the ammeter reads correctly, but the voltmeter measures the voltage across both resistor and ammeter, not just across the resistor, so there is a small error since you assume that the voltmeter is just measuring the voltage across the resistor.

The first circuit produces significant errors when the current through the voltmeter is significant compared with the current through the resistor; the second produces significant errors when the potential difference across the ammeter is significant compared with the potential difference across the resistor.

Internal resistance

Measuring the voltage across a cell

- Set up the circuit shown in Figure 36.1.
- Use a digital voltmeter to measure the voltage across a cell as shown.
- Watch the voltmeter as you connect first one and then two and more lamps across the cell.

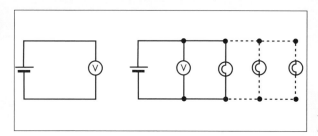

Figure 36.1   Measuring the voltage across a cell

E.m.f., terminal voltage and lost volts

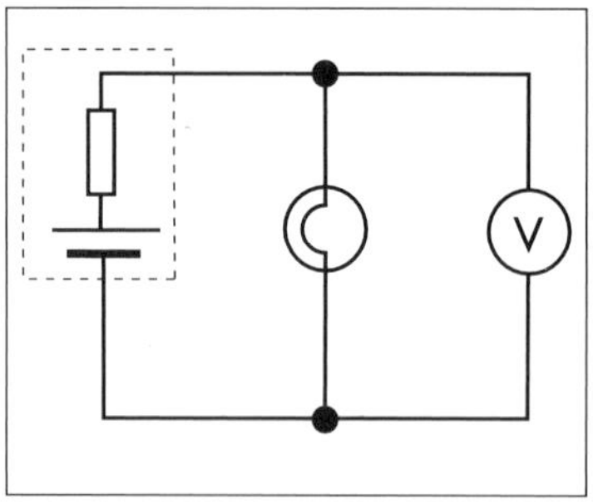

The voltage across the terminals of a cell is called the terminal voltage or **terminal p.d.** If you use a voltmeter that draws very little current to measure the terminal voltage when the cell is supplying no current, the voltmeter measures the cell's e.m.f.

The terminal p.d. of a cell is not constant; it depends on the current you draw from the cell. The larger the current you draw, the smaller the terminal voltage. You lose voltage as the current you draw increases. The **lost volts** is the difference between the e.m.f. and the terminal p.d.

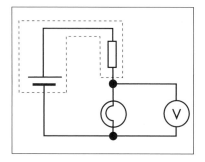

Figure 36.2   All sources of e.m.f. have internal resistance

Internal resistance

All sources of e.m.f. behave as if they have resistance connected in series with them (Figure 36.2). This resistance is called the **internal resistance**; it is resistance to the flow of current inside the power supply itself.

The internal resistance is part of the total resistance in the circuit. It behaves like any other resistance in the circuit. It needs a voltage across it to push current through it. But internal resistance is part of the power supply, and though you can represent it on a diagram as a separate resistance (Figure 36.3), you can't get at it to measure it directly. As current flows through the cell, there is a voltage drop across the internal resistance. This voltage drop is the lost volts when you draw current from the cell.

Figure 36.3   It is helpful to consider the internal resistance as part of the external circuit

Calculating internal resistance

The lost volts is equal to the difference between the e.m.f. and the terminal p.d. That is

lost volts = e.m.f. − terminal p.d.

or, in symbols,

lost volts = $E - V$

$E = \text{lost volts} + V$

But voltage = current × resistance. So if the internal resistance is r, and the current that flows is I, the lost voltage is equal to Ir. So

$E = Ir + V$

$V = E - Ir$

$V = (-r)I + E$

If you plot a graph of V against I, this will have slope equal to $-r$ and an intercept of E when $I = 0$.

Measuring internal resistance

- Connect a digital voltmeter alone to a cell to measure the e.m.f.
- Now connect, one at a time, a total of six lamps to the cell. Measure the terminal voltage and current through the cell as shown in Figure 36.4.
- Plot a graph of V against I. Find the internal resistance from the gradient and the e.m.f. from the intercept on the V axis (Figure 36.5).

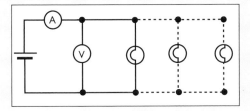

Figure 36.4   Use this circuit to measure internal resistance

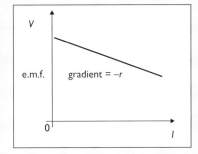

Figure 36.5   Graph of V against I to find internal resistance and e.m.f.

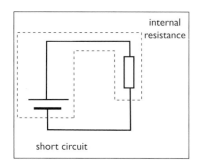

Figure 36.6   *The only resistance in this circuit is the internal resistance*

Figure 36.7   *When new, the internal resistance of this AA cell is about 0.5 Ω*

Energy, e.m.f and terminal voltage

The cell's e.m.f. does work on both the internal resistance and the external load. The **e.m.f.** of the cell is the total work done by the cell (including work done on the internal resistance) per coulomb of charge that flows.

$$\text{e.m.f.} = \frac{\text{total work done}}{\text{charge}}$$

Similarly, the terminal voltage or **terminal p.d.** is the work done on the external circuit per coulomb of charge that flows.

$$\text{terminal p.d.} = \frac{\text{work done on external circuit}}{\text{change}}$$

The units of e.m.f. and terminal p.d. follow from these definitions. They are joules per coulomb (J C^{-1}) = volts (V).

Short-circuit current

When you short-circuit a power supply by connecting the terminals together with a low resistance, the only significant resistance in the circuit may be the internal resistance of the power supply (Figure 36.6). In this case

current = e.m.f./internal resistance = E/r

For a new 1.5 V AA-size dry cell (Figure 36.7), the short-circuit current may be about 3 A. So the internal resistance

$r = E$

$I = 1.5$ V

3 A = 0.5 Ω

It is safe to short-circuit many small power supplies very briefly, because the internal resistances are usually large enough to prevent damage either to the power supply or to the short-circuiting components. But certain rechargeable cells, such as nickel–cadmium cells and lead–acid car batteries, have a very low internal resistance. They can provide dangerously large short-circuit currents.

Usually you want the internal resistance of a power supply to be low, so that it can supply large currents with little energy wasted in the supply. A car battery needs to supply perhaps 200 A. So it needs to have a very low internal resistance indeed.

On the other hand, it is sometimes an advantage to have a large internal resistance, for instance in a high-voltage power supply to prevent it supplying dangerously large currents.

Charging a capacitor

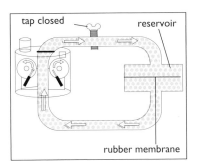

Figure 37.1 *An uncharged ball reservoir*

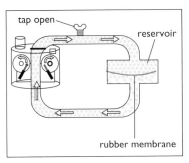

Figure 37.2 *A charged ball reservoir. As the reservoir charges, balls enter the top part and leave the bottom*

Charging a reservoir

Figure 37.1 shows a reservoir of balls that can store energy. The engine pushes balls into the top half, the rubber membrane stretches, and this pushes balls out of the bottom half. The charged reservoir doesn't really store balls; it just has more balls in the top and fewer balls in the bottom (Figure 37.2). If you connect the charged reservoir to a load, the membrane will push balls from the top part of the reservoir to the bottom part (Figure 37.3), powering the load for a short time.

An electrical reservoir

A **capacitor** is an electrical reservoir. It consists of two metal plates separated from each other by an insulating material. A wire from each plate connects the capacitor to the circuit. The circuit symbol shown in Figure 37.4 represents this structure. In practice, the metal plates are usually made of thin foil. They are often made in long strips with a thin insulator in between and rolled up into a cylinder resembling something like a Swiss-roll.

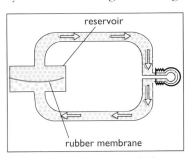

Figure 37.3 *The reservoir discharges through the load*

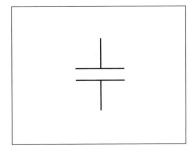

Figure 37.4 *The circuit symbol for a capacitor*

Monitoring the current in a capacitor circuit

- Connect a 1000 µF capacitor in series with a resistor and a battery pack, and a microammeter to record the current flow (Figure 37.5).
- Use wire W to short out the capacitor as shown by the dotted line. This effectively removes the capacitor from the circuit. Record the values of current, voltage and resistance and check that they agree with each other.
- Now remove one end of the shorting lead and observe the reading on the ammeter. Record the current every 5 s, starting from when the shorting lead was removed until the current has fallen to 5 per cent of its starting value. Plot a graph of current against time.
- Repeat the experiment with the microammeter connected at point B in the circuit. Plot another graph on the same axes.
- Now change the charging resistance, first to 220 kΩ and then to 470 kΩ. For each resistor, repeat the experiment.

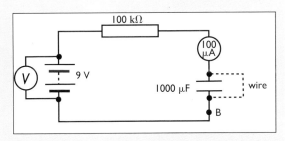

Figure 37.5 *Measuring the current in a capacitor circuit*

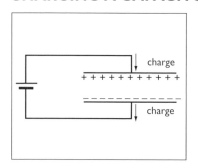

Figure 37.6 You can describe charging the capacitor in terms of the flow of positive charge

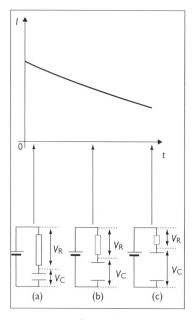

Figure 37.7 Change of current with time when charging a capacitor

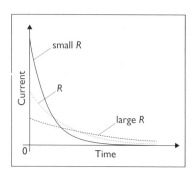

Figure 37.8 If you decrease the resistance in the charging circuit, you will increase the charging current. It then takes less time for the same charge to flow

Current in a capacitor circuit

You might be surprised that any current can flow in a series circuit containing a capacitor. After all, there is an insulating gap between the two plates and certainly no charge can flow through it. But the capacitor works like the ball reservoir. The battery draws charge from one plate and transfers an equal charge to the other plate without any charge going directly from one plate to the other (Figure 37.6).

At any instant the current through each lead of the capacitor is the same. This shows that an equal quantity of charge is going on to one of the capacitor's plates as is leaving the other.

A charged capacitor has extra charge on one plate and an equal shortage on the other. Just like the number of balls in the reservoir in Figures 37.1 and 37.2, the total charge within the capacitor remains the same. Charge is not actually stored, but moved from one place to another.

Why does the current change with time?

Kirchhoff's second law tells you that the voltage across the battery is equal to the voltage across the resistor plus the voltage across the capacitor:

$$V_{battery} = V_{resistor} + V_{capacitor}$$

At the beginning, when the capacitor is uncharged, the voltage across its plates is zero, so the voltage across the resistor is equal to the voltage across the battery (Figure 37.7a). The battery voltage is constant. As the capacitor charges, the voltage across it increases, and the voltage across the resistor decreases. This means that the current through the resistor, and therefore the whole circuit, decreases (Figure 37.7b). Eventually, when the capacitor is fully charged, the voltage across the capacitor is equal to the battery voltage. There is no voltage across the resistor and so no current in the circuit (Figure 37.7c).

Charging quickly or slowly

At the beginning, the capacitor is uncharged and has no voltage across it. So all the voltage across the resistance is the battery voltage. Therefore the initial current is

$$I_{max} = V_{resistor}/R = V_{battery}/R$$

As the capacitor charges up, the voltage across the resistor decreases.

Figure 37.8 shows three different graphs using the same battery and capacitor with three different charging resistances. Notice how the charging current is greater and the charging time is less for a smaller resistance.

Storing charge and energy

The meaning of capacitance

Capacitance is the ability of a component to store charge. But this can be misleading. The total charge at all times on a capacitor is zero; when it is charged, it holds equal amounts of positive and negative charges. Figure 38.1 shows a capacitor in which a charge Q is displaced from one plate to the other. The charge stored is said to be Q. As you can see, this means that the charge on the positive plate is $+Q$ and the charge on the negative plate is $-Q$. The quantity of charge Q that is displaced determines the value of its capacitance.

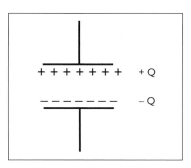

Figure 38.1   When a capacitor is charged, charge is displaced from one plate to another

Finding the quantity of charge on each plate

Figure 38.2 shows a current–time graph for a capacitor charging. When a current I flows onto a capacitor for a short time Δt, the charge $\Delta Q = I\Delta t$. This is the shaded area of the graph.

The total charge that flows is the total area under the curve. This is true for any current–time graph. You can find the charge stored by a capacitor by plotting a current–time graph and determining the area under the curve.

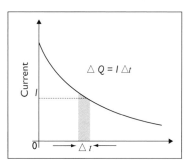

Figure 38.2   The shaded area is the charge flowing in time Δt

The definition of capacitance

The charge displaced Q is directly proportional to the charging potential difference V. If you plot a graph of charge against voltage, you get a straight line through the origin (Figure 38.4). The constant of proportionality between Q and V (and the gradient of the Q–V graph) is the capacitance, which is defined by the following equation:

Measuring the area under a current–time graph

- Use the experiment 'Monitoring the current in a capacitor circuit' in Chapter 37 to plot a current–time graph for a capacitor of 1000 μF charged to 3 V through a 100 kΩ resistor.
- Determine the charge that flows by finding the area under the curve as is done in Figure 38.3.
- Repeat the charging experiment for 4.5 V and 6 V.
- For each experiment, divide the charge by the voltage and compare your figures.

Figure 38.3   Calculating the area under a current–time graph: first choose a convenient size of square to count up the area; count up the number of squares, calling each significant part-square a half; calculate the charge represented by one square, and multiply this by the number of squares to find the total charge

```
                    4 x whole square = 4
                    8 x half square = 4
                              total = 8

20 mA □      1 square =
       10 s  20 mA x 10 s = 200 m As = 200 m C
             8 sq = 200 m C x 8 = 1600 m C
```

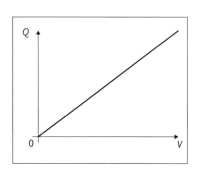

Figure 38.4   Graph of Q against V for a capacitor

$$\text{capacitance} = \frac{\text{charge displaced}}{\text{voltage across plates}}$$

$$C = \frac{Q}{V}$$

From this equation, you will see that the unit of capacitance is the coulomb per volt ($C\ V^{-1}$), called the farad (F). A farad is an extremely large capacitance and most values that you meet will be given in microfarads (μF), nanofarads (nF) or picofarads (pF).

Suppose the capacitor of Figure 38.4 had a charge of 1600 μC, and the charging voltage was 6 V. Then

capacitance = Q/V = 1600 μC/6 V = 270 μF, approximately

Another way of finding the charge on each plate

If you change the series resistance as a capacitor is being charged, you can control the charging current. A useful trick is to decrease the resistance as the capacitor charges to keep the charging current constant until the capacitor is fully charged. This produces the current–time graph shown in Figure 38.5. It is simple to calculate the charge that flows if the current is constant throughout the charging process: just multiply the current by the time. This is the same as finding the area under the rectangular current–time graph.

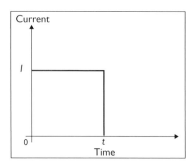

Figure 38.5   If you reduce the resistance while charging, you can keep the charging current constant

Charging a capacitor at a constant rate

- Set up the circuit in Figure 38.6. The 100 kΩ variable resistor allows you to control the charging current. Before completing the circuit, set the variable resistor to its maximum value, so that you don't pass a damagingly large current through the sensitive ammeter.
- Short the capacitor and adjust the variable resistor so that the maximum current is some convenient value on the meter.
- Remove the shorting lead and start timing; while you do so, use the variable resistor to maintain the current as near as possible to its starting value. Stop the clock when the resistor has reached its minimum value and the current drops rapidly.
- Repeat the experiment. Calculate the average time from several attempts and use this figure, together with the current and the charging voltage, to calculate the capacitance.

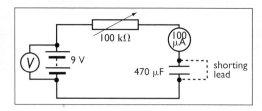

Figure 38.6   Charging a capacitor at a constant rate

How much energy can a capacitor store?

- Set up the circuit in Figure 38.7.
- Use six cells to charge your capacitor. Note the charging voltage and then discharge the capacitor through the resistor, using the joulemeter to measure the energy transferred.
- Repeat with a range of charging voltage.
- Plot a graph of energy against voltage squared and comment on the graph.
- Repeat the experiment with twice the capacitance.

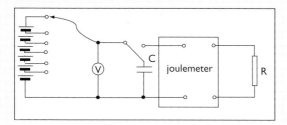

Figure 38.7   Use a joulemeter to measure how much energy a capacitor can store

Calculating energy stored

Figure 38.8 shows a graph of voltage against charge. Like the graph of charge against voltage in Figure 38.4, it is a straight line through the origin, but note that the axes are the other way round. Remember that voltage is the work done per unit charge, measured in joules per coulomb. So when a power supply adds a small amount of charge ΔQ to a capacitor at a voltage V, then the work done is $V\Delta Q$. This is equal to the shaded area on the graph.

The total work done charging the capacitor is equal to the areas of all the vertical strips, the total area under the graph. Since the graph is a straight line, the total work done W is simply the area of a triangle and is given by the equation

$$W = \tfrac{1}{2}QV$$

You can combine this equation with that which defines capacitance ($C = Q/V$) to produce two alternative expressions:

$$W = \tfrac{1}{2}CV^2 \quad \text{and} \qquad W = \tfrac{1}{2}Q^2/C$$

The work done by a supply as it puts a charge Q onto a capacitor is QV. The capacitor stores $\tfrac{1}{2}QV$; the remainder is dissipated in the circuit resistances as the capacitor charges. When the capacitor discharges, the $\tfrac{1}{2}QV$ that is stored is dissipated in the circuit through which the capacitor discharges. You should not be surprised that the same amount of energy is dissipated on charging and discharging. If both take place through the same resistance, both result from the charging current being the same as the discharging current and flowing for the same time, but in the opposite direction.

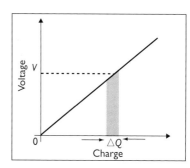

Figure 38.8   Graph of voltage against charge for a capacitor to measure energy stored

Capacitor combinations

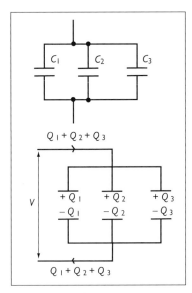

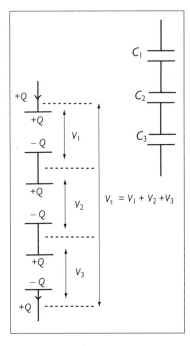

Figure 39.1 When capacitors are connected in parallel, the total charge that flows is equal to the sum of the charges for each capacitor

Figure 39.2 When capacitors are connected in series, the voltage across the whole is equal to the sum of the voltages across each capacitor

Capacitors in parallel

When you connect capacitors in parallel (Figure 39.1), the capacitances add up. The voltage across each capacitor is the same and the amount of charge on the plates of each capacitor is determined by its capacitance.

The single capacitor that could replace this arrangement would have to hold an amount of charge on its plates equal to that held by all three capacitors when it has the same potential difference across it. So

$$Q_t = Q_1 + Q_2 + Q_3$$

But since $Q_1 = C_1 V$, $Q_2 = C_2 V$ and $Q_3 = C_3 V$ we can write

$$\text{total charge} = C_1 V + C_2 V + C_3 V$$
$$= V(C_1 + C_2 + C_3)$$

and

$$\frac{\text{total charge}}{V} = C_1 + C_2 + C_3$$

This represents the capacitance that is equivalent to the parallel arrangement shown:

$$C_t = C_1 + C_2 + C_3$$

So if a 100 μF is connected in parallel with a 200 μF capacitor,

$$C_t = C_1 + C_2 = 100 \text{ μF} + 200 \text{ μF} = 300 \text{ μF}$$

Capacitors in series

When you connect capacitors in series, the total capacitance is *less* than each individual capacitance.

The three capacitors in Figure 39.2 form part of a series circuit. At any instant, the current in all the connecting leads must be the same. You would get the same current–time graph wherever you connected an ammeter into the circuit. Since $\Delta Q = I \Delta t$, each capacitor must have the same displaced charge. The voltage across each capacitor is determined by its capacitance.

The single capacitor that could replace this arrangement would have to hold this amount of charge on its plates when it has the total potential difference of the three individual capacitors across it. So

$$V_t = V_1 + V_2 + V_3$$

But since $V_1 = Q/C_1$, $V_2 = Q/C_2$, $V_3 = Q/C_3$ and we have

$$Q/C_t = \frac{Q}{C_1} + \frac{Q}{C_2} + \frac{Q}{C_3}$$

and

$$\frac{1}{C_t} = \frac{1}{C_1} + \frac{1}{C_2} + \frac{1}{C_3}$$

If you connect a capacitance of 100 μF in parallel with a capacitance of 200 μF,

$$\frac{1}{C_t} = \frac{1}{C_1} + \frac{1}{C_2}$$

$$\frac{1}{C_t} = \frac{1}{100\ \mu F} + \frac{1}{200\ \mu F}$$

$$\frac{1}{C_t} = \frac{200 + 100}{100 \times 200\ \mu F}$$

$$\frac{1}{C_t} = \frac{300}{100 \times 200\ \mu F}$$

$$C_t = \frac{100 \times 200\ \mu F}{300} = 67\mu F$$

Complete the circuit below to show the capacitors connected in parallel.

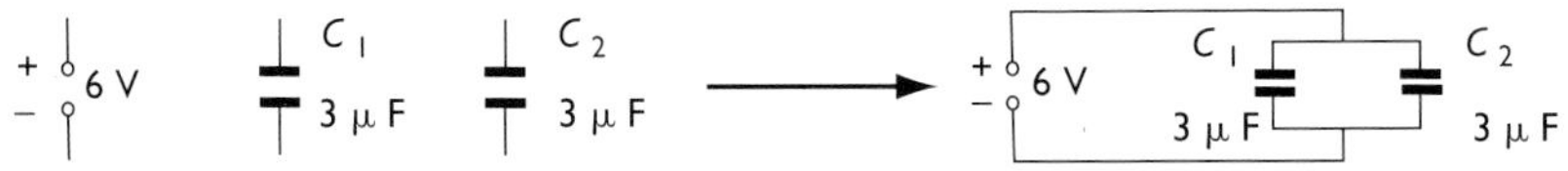

Complete the circuit below to show the capacitors connectes in series.

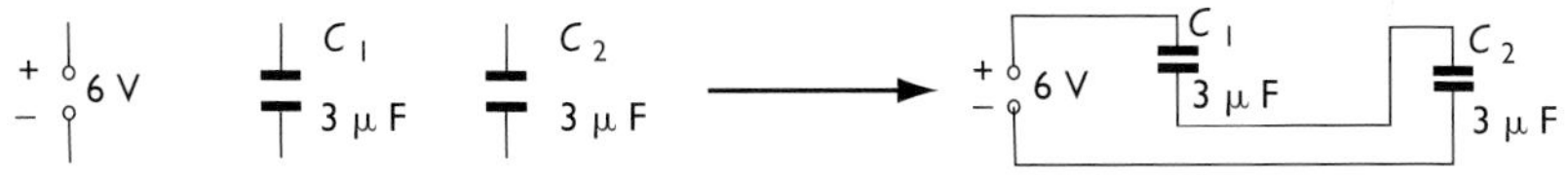

Use the information in the diagrams to complete the following table.

Capacitors in parallel	Charge on C_1	$Q_1 = C_1 V = 3\ \mu F \times 6V = 18\ \mu C$
	Energy stored in C_1 when fully charged	$W_1 = \frac{1}{2}C_1V^2 = \frac{1}{2} \times 3\ \mu F \times 36\ V^2$ $= 54\ \mu J$
Capacitors in in series	Charge on C_2	Voltage across $C_2 = \frac{1}{2} \times 6\ V = 3\ V$ $Q_2 = C_2 V_2 = 3\ \mu F \times 3V = 9\ \mu C$
	Working done by power supply as it charges both capacitors	$9\ \mu C$ flows through 6 V supply $W = Q\ V = 9\ \mu C \times 6\ V = 54\ \mu J$

Practice questions

Chapter 1

1.1 List the six *base quantities* that you will be using in your A-level course. Give the unit of each of these quantities.

1.2 What is meant by a *derived unit*? Write down three derived units and express them in base units.

1.3 Write down the word equation for *acceleration*. Use this equation to show that the unit of acceleration is m s^{-2}.

1.4 Show that the equations $v = u + at$ and $v = 2u + \frac{1}{4}at$ are both homogeneous. Explain why they need not be correct.

Chapter 2

2.1 Distinguish between a *scalar* and a *vector* quantity. Consider the following quantities: acceleration, distance, energy, weight, volume, displacement, speed, momentum, mass, velocity, force, power. Which are scalars and which are vectors?

2.2 A cyclist travels to work at an average speed of 3 m s^{-1} and returns home for tea at an average speed of 9 m s^{-1}. Calculate her average speed for the whole journey. [Think carefully!]

2.3 A launch leaves the bank of a river and heads directly for the opposite bank at a velocity of 8 m s^{-1}. The water is moving at right angles to the launch's velocity at a velocity of 2 m s^{-1}. Find the resultant velocity of the launch and state the actual direction in which it moves.

2.4 Describe how to monitor the acceleration of a trolley. Show clearly how you calculate the acceleration.

Chapter 3

3.1 Use the distance–time graph to find: (a) how far the body has moved after 10 s, (b) how long the body takes to travel 8 m, (c) the average speed of the body after 15 s, and (d) its instantaneous speed when $t = 5$ s.

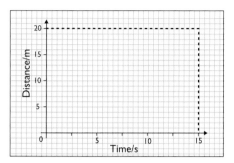

3.2 Use the velocity – time graph to find: (a) the acceleration during the first six seconds, (b) the distance travelled during this acceleration, (c) the total distance covered between 'stops', and (d) the average speed during the 22 second journey.

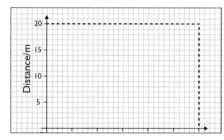

3.3 An object accelerates from rest with a constant acceleration of 4 m s^{-2}. Sketch the shape of the following graphs for the first 3 seconds of its journey and label both axes with accurate scales:
(a) acceleration against time; (b) velocity against time; and (c) displacement against time.

3.4 Draw a velocity–time graph for a ball thrown vertically upwards and caught at the same horizontal level. Take the upward direction as positive and ignore the effect of air resistance. Explain how you would use your graph to obtain the acceleration of gravity.

Chapter 4

4.1 A stone dropped from rest down a well takes 1.9 s to hit the surface of the water. Calculate the depth of the well.

4.2 An electron moving at a speed of 1×10^5 m s^{-1} travels 20 cm through an electric field. It leaves in the same direction with a speed of 9×10^5 m s^{-1}. Find: (a) the acceleration of the electron while it is in the electric field, and (b) the time in the field.

4.3 How long will it take a pebble dropped from rest from a 30 m high cliff to reach the bottom? Calculate the pebble's speed immediately prior to striking the ground.

4.4 Calculate the speed with which a bullet must be fired vertically in order to reach a height of 200 m. How long will the bullet be in the air? What is the difference between the total distance travelled by the bullet and its final displacement?

Chapter 5

5.1 Describe how to determine the acceleration of a freely falling object. Include a labelled diagram of the apparatus and show how to calculate the acceleration from a suitable straight-line graph.

5.2 A rocket launched vertically rises for 6 s with a uniform acceleration of 150 m s^{-2}, after which time it is only acted upon by gravitational forces (assumed constant). Calculate the maximum speed. How long after its launch does the rocket reach its maximum height? Calculate the maximum height. Sketch acceleration–time and velocity–time graphs for the upward motion of the rocket.

5.3 A dart leaves the thrower's hand horizontally at a height of 1.9 m above the ground. It strikes a board 3 m away at a height of 1.5 m above the ground. Calculate: (a) the time taken by the dart to reach the board, and (b) the horizontal velocity with which the dart leaves the hand of the thrower.

Chapter 6

6.1 Explain the term *resultant force*. An object is acted upon by two forces of 8 N and 12 N. Calculate the size of both the maximum and the minimum resultant force which can act on this object, explaining how the two forces must act to achieve each of these.

6.2 Give two ways in which the motion of a body would indicate that the resultant force acting on it was zero.

6.3 Write down *Newton's first law* of motion.

6.4 How do car inertia-reel seat belts work?

Chapter 7

7.1 Describe how to investigate the relationship between the resultant force acting on a body and its acceleration.

7.2 Write down *Newton's second law* of motion. Show how this law leads to a definition of the newton. Write down this definition.

7.3 In a time of 10 s, a car of mass 1200 kg accelerates from rest to a speed of 40 m s^{-1} along a horizontal road. Calculate: (a) its average acceleration, and (b) the average resultant force.

7.4 Calculate the acceleration when a horizontal force of 150 N pushes a block of mass 30 kg across the top of a bench, assuming that: (a) the surfaces are frictionless, and (b) a frictional force of 30 N acts between the two surfaces.

Chapter 8

8.1 Write down *Newton's third law* of motion.

8.2 Explain why none of the pairs of forces a to d shown in the diagram can be Newton's third-law pairs.

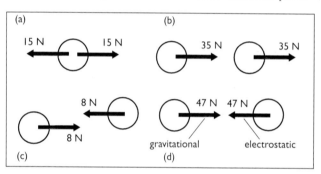

8.3 Write down two examples of Newton's third-law force pairs and use them to illustrate the characteristics of a Newton III pair.

Chapter 9

9.1 Give three examples of non-contact forces.

9.2 How do contact forces arise?

9.3 List the four types of force.

Chapter 10

10.1 Draw a free-body force diagram for a body moving at 45 m s^{-1} in outer space a long way from planets.

10.2 A body is near a planet. Draw free-body force diagrams for both the body and the planet. What are the effects of the forces on (a) the body and (b) the planet?

PRACTICE QUESTIONS

10.3 Fred pushes Joe left with a contact force of 40 N. Identify the force that forms a Newton's third-law pair with this force.

10.4 A man is standing on a planet. Draw a situation diagram and free-body force diagrams for both the man and the planet.

10.5 When this book rests on a table, it has equal and opposite vertical forces acting on it. Outline the major differences between these two forces and a Newton's third-law pair of forces.

Chapter 11

11.1 Two perpendicular forces of 14 N and 9 N act together on an object. Use a scale drawing to find the magnitude and direction of the resultant. Check your answers by calculation. Why is the object not in equilibrium?

11.2 Calculate the resultant of 35 N north and 86 N south-west.

11.3 A small object has four forces pulling on it from different directions in the same plane. Find the magnitude and direction of the resultant of the three forces shown. The object is in equilibrium. Give the size and direction of the fourth force.

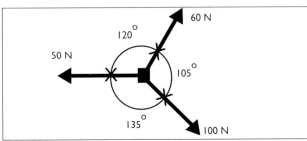

11.4 Calculate the vertical and horizontal components of a force of 279 MN acting at 38° to the vertical.

Chapter 12

12.1 A book is resting on a table. The table is resting on a planet. Draw free-body force diagrams for the book, table and planet.

12.2 A car is driven along a straight road at a steady speed. Draw a free-body force diagram for the car. What can you say about the forces on the car?

12.3 A man pushes a box along the ground. Draw a free-body force diagram for the box. What can you say about the forces on the box if (a) the box is moving at a steady speed and (b) the box is accelerating?

12.4 Draw a free-body force diagram for an aircraft flying horizontally at a steady speed. What can you say about these forces? Draw another free-body force diagram for the aircraft now diving at a steady speed at an angle of 30° to the horizontal. What can you now say about the forces on the aircraft?

Chapter 13

13.1 What is the *moment* of a force? Calculate the moment of the forces about the point P in cases a and b.

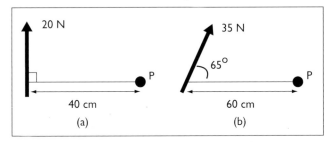

13.2 A driver applies 18 N with each hand at opposite sides of the steering wheel to produce the maximum turning effect. Sketch a diagram of the steering wheel showing clearly the two forces acting on it. If the steering wheel has a radius of 18 cm, calculate the moment of these two forces.

13.3 What is the *centre of gravity* of a body. How would you locate the position of the centre of gravity of an irregular object.

13.4 A clampstand is balanced as shown. The centre of gravity, G, is 8 cm from the pivot. The weight *W* and the distance *x* are varied to keep the stand balanced.

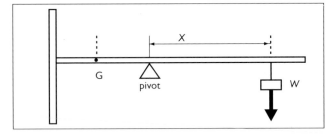

Corresponding readings of *W* and *x* are recorded.

W/N	x/cm
2.0	52
3.0	35
4.0	26
5.0	21
6.0	17
7.0	15
8.0	13

Plot a graph of W (y-axis) against $1/x$ (x-axis). Draw the (straight) line of best fit. Using your graph, calculate the weight of the clampstand. What is the mass of the clampstand?

Chapter 14

14.1   A uniform rod of length 3 m and weight 150 N is suspended horizontally by a vertical wire attached at 50 cm from one end and another attached at 30 cm from the other end. Calculate the tension in each wire.

14.2   A uniform horizontal rod AB is 120 cm long and weighs 250 N. It is supported by two vertical wires, one 10 cm from A and the other 20 cm from B. Loads of 100 N and 350 N hang from the rod at distances of 50 cm and 100 cm respectively from A. Calculate the tension in each wire.

14.3   A uniform sphere of weight 25 N is supported by a string. A horizontal force pulls the sphere to one side so that the string makes an angle of 30° with the vertical. Draw and label a free-body force diagram for the sphere. By considering only the vertical force components, calculate the tension in the string. Then find the horizontal force.

14.4   The diagram shows a sign, weight 90 N, attached to one end of a uniform rod, the other end of which is hinged to the wall. The length of the rod is 1.5 m and its weight is 30 N. The wire keeps the rod horizontal. Calculate (a) the tension in the wire, and (b) the vertical and horizontal forces exerted by the hinge.

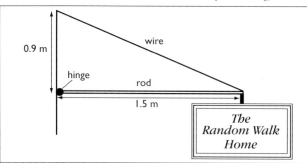

Chapter 15

15.1   Is *momentum* a scalar or a vector quantity? Calculate the momentum of a toy train of mass 1600 g travelling at 25 cm s^{-1}.

15.2   A bullet of mass 20 g moving at 300 m s^{-1} embeds in a stationary wooden block of mass 3980 g. Calculate their combined speed after impact.

15.3   An ice skater, mass 65 kg, moving at 7 m s^{-1}, collides head-on with another skater, mass 45 kg, moving at 6 m s^{-1}. Calculate their speed and direction as they move off together.

15.4   A boy throws a 100 g stone horizontally at a speed of 6 m s^{-1}. A squirrel, mass 500 g, sitting on ice, catches the stone and then throws it back horizontally at 2 m s^{-1}. Find: (a) the initial momentum of the stone, (b) the speed of the squirrel when it has caught the stone, and (c) the speed of the squirrel after it has thrown the stone back.

Chapter 16

16.1   Write down a word equation for *impulse*. What unit of impulse derives directly from this equation? Rewrite this unit in terms of base units only. What other physical quantity has the same unit as impulse?

16.2   A stationary snooker ball of mass 150 g is hit by a cue which exerts an average force of 60 N on it. The duration of the impact is 8 ms. Calculate: (a) the impulse of the force exerted by the cue, and (b) the speed at which the snooker ball leaves the cue.

16.3   A car travelling at 30 m s^{-1} collides with a wall and is brought to rest in 0.5 s. The mass of the car and occupants is 900 kg. Calculate: (a) the change in the momentum of the car during its collision with the wall, (b) the impulse that the wall exerts on the car during the collision, and (c) the average force exerted by the wall on the car during the collision.

16.4   In an experiment to find the average force exerted by a hammer when it is knocking a nail into a block of wood, the measurements shown in the table were taken.

Speed of hammer just before it hits the nail	8 m s^{-1}
Speed of hammer *rebounding* from the nail	2 m s^{-1}
Mass of hammer head	300 g
Time of contact between the hammer and the nail	12 ms

(a) Calculate the change in the momentum of the hammer head. (b) What impulse was exerted on the nail by the hammer head? (c) Calculate the average force exerted by the hammer head while it is in contact with the nail. (d) How would you attempt to measure the time of contact in the above experiment?

PRACTICE QUESTIONS

Chapter 17

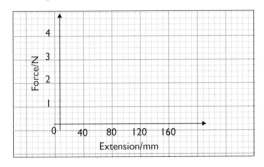

17.1   Use the graph to find: (a) the work done in stretching the spring from its original length to an extension of 60 mm; and (b) the work done in increasing the extension of the spring from 40 mm to 140 mm.

17.2   A man of mass 80 kg takes one minute to climb up a staircase 21 m high. Doing this he travels a total distance of 36 m. Calculate: (a) his average speed, (b) his average velocity, (c) his average power, and (d) the total work he does.

17.3   A car has a power of 35 kW at a maximum speed of 144 km h^{-1}. Calculate the force acting against the motion of the car.

Chapter 18

18.1   Is *energy* a scalar or a vector quantity? Express the unit of energy in terms of base units. Calculate the kinetic energy of 600 g moving at 125 cm s^{-1}. If all this kinetic energy was converted into gravitational potential energy, find the vertical height through which the mass would rise.

18.2   A flea has a mass of 0.5 mg. It jumps vertically upwards at 1.5 m s^{-1}. Calculate: (a) its kinetic energy as it leaves the ground, and (b) the maximum height it reaches.

Chapter 19

19.1   A trolley of mass 4 kg is initially at rest on a friction-compensated runway. A string attached to this trolley passes over a frictionless pulley at the bottom of the runway and is tied to a 1 kg mass which is 25 cm above the ground. The trolley is released. Calculate: (a) the potential energy lost by the mass falling to the ground, and (b) the speed of the trolley and mass just before the mass hits the ground.

19.2   What is the *internal energy* of a body? Give some examples of how internal energy may be increased.

19.3   What is meant by *efficiency*? A 60 W light bulb is 2% efficient as a light source. How much power does it give out as light? What happens to the rest of the input?

Chapter 20

20.1   What do *elastic* and *inelastic* collisions have in common? What is different for these two types of collision?

20.2   A railway truck of mass 4×10^4 kg moves at 3 m s^{-1} towards a stationary truck of mass 2×10^4 kg. The trucks collide and join. Calculate the total momentum of the two trucks before the collision. What is the total momentum of the two trucks both before and after the collision. Compare the kinetic energy after the collision with that before the collision. Why does your answer not contradict the law of conservation of energy?

Chapter 21

21.1   Why is an object accelerating if it is moving at a constant speed along a circular path? The force required to produce this acceleration is given by the equation $F = mv^2/r$. Show that this equation is homogeneous.

21.2   A car travels around a circular bend of radius 1 km at a constant speed of 108 km h^{-1}. Calculate its angular velocity in SI units.

21.3   The diagram shows the starting position of the tape in a 'C90' audio cassette. The empty spool (B) has a diameter of 21 mm while that of the full spool (A) is 51 mm. The tape travels from spool A to spool B at a constant speed of 47.6 mm s^{-1}, taking exactly 45 minutes to empty spool A. Calculate: (a) the total length of tape in the cassette, and (b) the initial angular velocities of the two spools. (c) How will the motion of the two spools vary as the tape is being played?

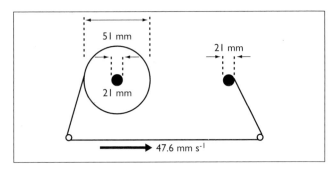

21.4 A 0.5 kg stone on the end of a 2 m length of string is whirled round in a horizontal circle on a level frictionless table. The stone moves at a constant speed of 7 m s^{-1}. Calculate: (a) the stone's acceleration, stating its direction, (b) the tension in the string, and (c) the work done on the stone by the tension during 10 revolutions, explaining your answer.

Chapter 22

22.1 A conical pendulum consists of a 510 g bob on a 60 cm string. The bob is rotated in a horizontal circle with the string at 30° to the vertical. Draw a free-body force diagram for the bob. Calculate: (a) the tension in the string, (b) the speed of the bob, and (c) the period of its motion.

22.2 The graph shows how the tension in a string varies with time. A mass is on the end of the string following a vertical circular path of radius 70 cm at a constant speed. Why does the tension in the string vary? Use the graph to find: (a) the weight of the mass used, and (b) the speed at which the mass is moving.

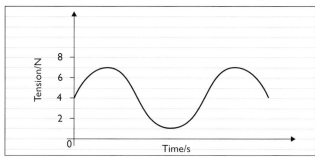

22.3 What is the difference between *weightlessness* and *apparent weightlessness*?

Chapter 23

23.1 What is the difference between a *cell* and a *battery*?

23.2 What is an *electric current*?

23.3 Draw 'engine diagrams' for circuits A to D. Predict what will happen. In which circuits will the engine run out of fuel fastest?

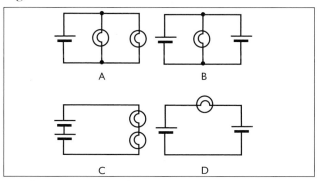

Chapter 24

24.1 Two objects, A and B, are initially uncharged. A positive charge of 4 nC flows from A to B. What is the charge on each object?

24.2 Give the units of *charge* and *current*. What is the relationship between them?

24.3 What charge flows when a current of (a) 3 A flows for 4 s, (b) 7 A flows for 8 min, and (c) 0.25 A flows for 2 h?

24.4 What current flows when a charge of (a) 700 C passes a point in 35 s, and (b) 3600 C passes a point in 3 min?

24.5 A current of 4.5 A flows in a car headlamp bulb for 20 minutes. Calculate the charge that passes through the filament. How many electrons drift past any given point in the filament? [Electronic charge = 1.6×10^{-19} C]

Chapter 25

25.1 Give typical values for the current through the following components in normal operation: torch bulb, LED, small motor, buzzer, mains lamp, electric kettle.

25.2 Calculate the unknown currents I_1 to I_9 in the circuits A to D.

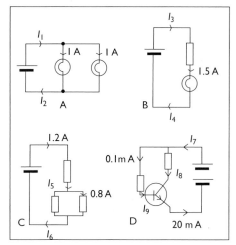

Chapter 26

26.1 The atomic radius of aluminium is 0.125 nm. Calculate approximately the number of atoms per unit volume.

26.2 A copper wire, as used for house mains wiring, has a cross-sectional area of 2.5 mm^2 and carries a maximum current of 25 A. The charge is carried by electrons, of which there are about 7×10^{28} per metre cubed. The charge on an electron is $(-)1.6 \times 10^{-19}$ C. Calculate the drift speed of the electrons when the wire is carrying its maximum current.

Chapter 27

27.1 Three identical lamps are connected in parallel to a battery. Draw a circuit diagram of the arrangement. The current through one lamp is 800 mA. Mark on all wires on your diagram the value of the current in that wire.

27.2 Design a circuit that will switch on a warning lamp, which takes a small current, when the temperature of a sensor becomes too high.

27.3 An electric fire and a lamp are both connected to the mains supply. Draw a circuit diagram for this arrangement. The fire takes a current of 12 A and the lamp 0.4 A. Mark on your diagram the value of the current in each wire.

27.4 Design a circuit that uses an LDR to make a light meter.

Chapter 28

28.1 Copy the circuit diagram and show how you would use a voltmeter to measure all the voltages. Label the positive terminal of the voltmeter in each case.

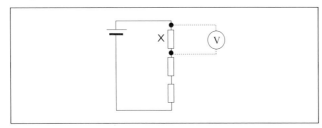

28.2 What are the unknown voltages in the circuits shown?

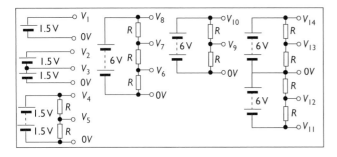

Chapter 29

29.1 How many joules of energy does a 9 volt battery supply when (a) a charge of 15 coulombs flows through it, and (b) a current of 0.5 amps flows through it for 2 minutes?

29.2 A heater supplies 36 000 joules of energy in 10 minutes when a current of 3 amperes flows. (a) How much energy is produced each second? (b) How much charge flows through the heater each second? (c) How much energy is produced each time a coulomb flows through the heater?

29.3 The power of a torch bulb is 0.75 W when the current through it is 0.3 A. What is the p.d. across it?

29.4 The energy transfer by a small d.c. generator was 0.3 MJ driving a current of 2.5 A for 10 minutes. How much charge flows in this time? What is the e.m.f. of the generator?

Chapter 31

31.1 What is *Kirchhoff's second law*? Explain, with reference to a physical principle, why it is reasonable to expect the sum of the e.m.f.'s to equal the sum of the p.d.'s.

31.2 Draw two different electrical circuits, each containing a 12 volt battery and four 1000 ohm resistors. Estimate sensible values for the voltages across each component and label the diagrams with these voltages. Mark the direction of current flow in each wire.

Chapter 32

32.1 Express the *volt* and the *ohm* in terms of base units.

32.2 The combined resistance of two resistors is 120 Ω. One of the resistors has a resistance of 180 Ω. How are the two resistors connected? Calculate the resistance of the other resistor.

32.3 You are provided with three 18 Ω resistors which can be used individually, in pairs or in combinations involving all three. Sketch each of the seven possible resistor combinations, calculating the combined resistance in each case.

Chapter 33

33.1 Calculate the resistance of 100 m of mains cable made from wires having a cross-sectional area of 1.5 mm². What would the voltage drop in that cable be if the current through it were 13 A?

33.2 For each of the following materials, explain whether you would expect their *resistivity* to rise or fall as the temperature increases: copper, carbon, glass, iron, paraffin wax, silicon.

33.3 Sketch graphs to show how the resistance varies with temperature for (a) a tungsten filament lamp, and (b) a n-t-c thermistor. Explain in terms of the conduction processes involved why the resistances vary in this way.

33.4 A n-t-c thermistor at room temperature has a resistance of 300 Ω. What current will flow in it when a voltage of 12 V is connected across it? How much power is generated by this current flowing through it? If the thermistor dissipates energy to its surroundings at a rate of 300 mW, what happens to (a) the thermistor's temperature, and (b) its resistance? What effect will this change in resistance have on the power generated within the thermistor?

Chapter 34

34.1 For the circuit shown, calculate: (a) the combined resistance of the parallel combination; (b) the total circuit resistance; (c) the current supplied by the battery; (d) the potential difference across the 360 Ω resistor; (e) the potential difference across the parallel combination; (f) the current flowing through the 600 Ω resistor; and (g) the current flowing through the 400 Ω resistor.

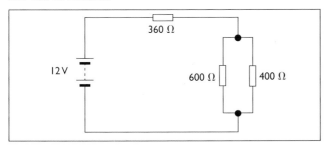

34.2 For the resistance network (a), calculate the total resistance between terminals KN, KL and LM. A second resistor network (b) is set up as shown. The resistances used are *x*, *y* and *z*. Write down expressions (in terms of

x, *y* and *z*) for the total resistance between terminals KN, KL and LM. The two resistor networks have identical electrical properties. Find the values of *x*, *y* and *z*.

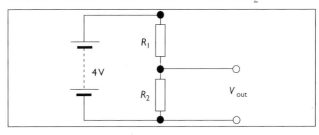

34.3 A light-dependent resistor is connected in series with a 900 Ω fixed resistor and a 5 V supply. The graph shows how the resistance of the LDR varies with the intensity of the light (measured in lux) falling on it. Use the graph to calculate the voltage across the 900 Ω resistor when the LDR is placed (a) in bright sunlight (1000 lux), and (b) 50 cm away from a 40 W bulb (90 lux).

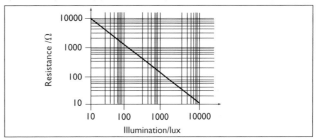

34.4 The circuit diagram shows a battery of e.m.f. 4 V and negligible internal resistance connected across a potential divider. What must happen to the output terminals to produce the maximum output current, I_{out}? Given that the output current must not exceed 0.5 A, calculate the resistance of R_1. The output potential difference V_{out} is found to be 3 V when the output current is 0.1 A. Calculate the resistance of R_2.

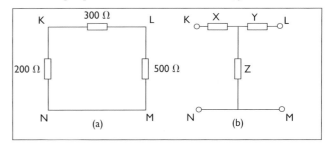

Chapter 35

35.1 State *Ohm's law*. Describe an experiment to test whether a conductor obeys Ohm's law.

PRACTICE QUESTIONS

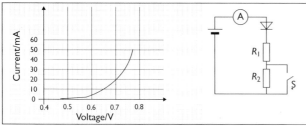

35.2 The graph shows the current–voltage characteristics for the diode in the circuit shown. The cell has an e.m.f. of 2.5 V. When S is closed, the current is 50 mA. Calculate R_1. When S is open, the current is 10 mA. Calculate R_2. What is the power dissipated in the diode when the switch S is closed?

Chapter 36

36.1 The battery in the circuit has an e.m.f. of 12 V and an internal resistance of 2 Ω. What is the reading on the voltmeter with switch S open? The switch S is now closed. Calculate the current flowing through the 4 Ω resistor. What is the terminal p.d. of the supply? Calculate the power dissipated in the internal resistance and the power dissipated in the external circuit.

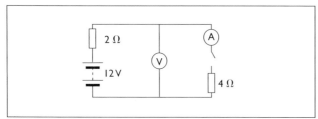

36.2 The data in the table were obtained from an experiment to measure the internal resistance of a cell. Use a graph to find the e.m.f. and the internal resistance of the cell.

Current/mA	Terminal p.d./V
100	1.48
200	1.32
300	1.15
400	0.99
500	0.83
600	0.67

36.3 A small torch bulb is rated at 4.5 V, 720 mW. What is its working resistance? Calculate the value of the series resistance needed for the bulb to operate normally from a 12 V supply with an internal resistance 4 Ω. The bulb operates normally when connected directly across another supply which has an e.m.f. of 6 V. What is the internal resistance of this supply?

36.4 A battery of e.m.f. of 9 V drives a current of 500 mA through a resistance of 12 Ω. What is the battery's internal resistance?

Chapter 37

37.1 How can a current flow in a circuit containing a capacitor in series with a resistor when no charge is able to pass directly between the capacitor's plates? Why does the current flowing in a capacitor circuit decrease with time? Why does a capacitor take a longer time to charge significantly when in series with a larger resistance?

37.2 Draw a circuit to measure how current varies with time for a capacitor charging from a 20 V supply through a 22 kΩ resistor. Sketch the current–time graph that would be obtained.

Chapter 38

38.1 Define *capacitance*. Express the unit of capacitance in terms of base units.

38.2 The following readings of current (μA) in a capacitor circuit were recorded at 10 s intervals: 80, 65, 52, 42, 34, 28, 22, 18, 15, 12, 10, 8, 6. Plot a graph of current against time and use it to find an approximate value for the charge on either plate. The resistor connected in series with the capacitor has a value of 50 kΩ. What is the voltage of the battery? Find an approximate value for this capacitance. If the same capacitor is charged with a constant current of 25 μA, how long will it take to charge it by the same amount?

38.3 Sketch current–time graphs on the same axes for a high- and a low-value capacitor charged by the same supply through identical resistors.

38.4 A capacitor stores 10 μC when charged from a 50 V supply. Calculate its capacitance and the energy stored.

Chapter 39

39.1 You are provided with three 500 μF capacitors which can be used individually, in pairs or in combinations involving all three. Sketch each of the possible capacitor combinations, calculating the combined capacitance in each case.

39.2 A 100 μF capacitor is in series with a 250 μF capacitor and a 6 V battery. Calculate the charge and potential difference for each capacitor.

Examination questions

1   The following list gives some quantities and units:

   coulomb   force   length   mole   newton   temperature interval

Identify those which are base quantities of the International (SI) System of Units.   [2]

The volt is a derived unit. Express the volt in terms of base units.   [3]

Explain the difference between scalar and vector quantities.   [2]

Is potential difference a scalar or vector quantity?   [1]

2   Kepler discovered that the orbital periods T of the planets about the Sun are related to their distances r from the Sun. From Newton's laws, the following relationship may be derived:

$$T^2 = \left(\frac{4\pi^2}{GM}\right) r^3$$

where M is the mass of the Sun.

Use the equation to find units for G in terms of base units.   [2]

3   A glass cylinder, 50 cm high, is filled with water. A small plastic sphere of radius r is released at the water surface and falls slowly to the bottom of the cylinder. It speeds up over the first few centimetres and falls the rest of the way at a constant downwards speed v. When the sphere is falling at constant speed the upward resistive force, $6\pi rkv$, equals the net downwards force F, i.e.

   $F = 6\pi rkv$

Find a unit for k in terms of base units.   [3]

With the aid of a diagram, describe how you would check whether or not the speed of the sphere is constant over the final 30 cm of its journey.   [4]

4   A student whose mass is 40 kg is an expert with a skateboard. He stands with his right foot on the board and pushes himself along a hard level surface with his left foot. The graph shows approximately how the horizontal force F exerted by his foot on the ground varies during the first few seconds.

Calculate the student's speed after 2 seconds, 4 seconds and 5.8 seconds.   [4]

Use these values to draw a speed–time graph for the skater's motion from $t = 0$ to t = 6 s.   [4]

Why does the time for which the student's left foot is in contact with the ground get shorter and shorter?   [2]

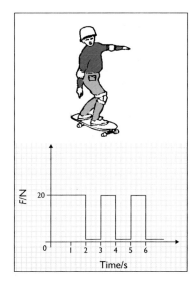

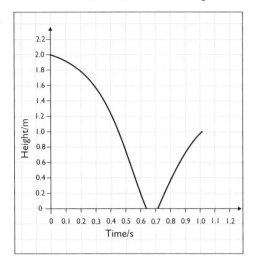

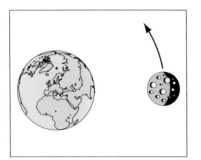

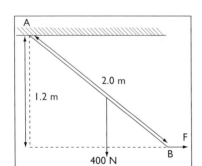

5 A rubber ball of mass 0.120 kg is dropped from a height of 2.00 m (measured from the bottom of the ball) on to a flat horizontal patch of hard soil. Calculate the speed of the ball when it hits the ground. [3]

The rubber ball loses speed each time it bounces. The graph shows how the height of the bottom of the ball varies with time during the first second of its motion.

Use the graph to show that the speed of the ball as it leaves the ground is approximately 4.7 m s^{-1}. [3]

Calculate the average force exerted by the ground on the ball while it is in contact with the ground. [4]

6 Draw a labelled diagram of the apparatus you would use to measure the acceleration of a body in free fall. [3]

List the measurements you would make and show how you would use them to calculate the acceleration. [5]

Identify and explain one precaution you would take to minimise the errors in your experiment. [2]

7 The diagram shows the Moon in its orbit about the Earth.

Draw and label two free-body force diagrams, one for the Earth and one for the Moon. Ignore the effects of any other bodies. [2]

State the four principal characteristics of a Newton's third-law pair of forces. [4]

8 Give a brief explanation of the term *centre of gravity*. [2]

The diagram shows a heavy uniform rod AB of length 2.0 m and of weight 400 N. It is hinged at A and held to one side by a horizontal force *F* acting at B.

Calculate the magnitude of the force *F* acting at B. [3]

State the magnitudes of the vertical and horizontal forces acting on the rod at A. Find the magnitude of the resultant. [4]

9 State Newton's second law of motion. [2]

A student says, incorrectly, 'Momentum is conserved completely in elastic collisions, but not in inelastic collisions.' Rewrite this sentence to make a correct statement about momentum conservation. [1]

In what circumstances is kinetic energy conserved in a collision? [1]

10 Define *work*. Write down a unit for work in terms of base units. Define *power*. Write down a unit for power in terms of base units. [4]

A small electric van is powered by a large 120 V battery. A force of 500 N is needed to drive it along a level road at a steady speed of 11 m s^{-1}. Calculate the power developed by the motor and the current flowing in the battery. [4]

11 The graph shows how the height above the ground of the top of a soft bouncing ball varies with time.

Describe briefly the principal energy changes which occur between the times t_A and t_B, t_B and t_C, t_C and t_D. [2+3+1]

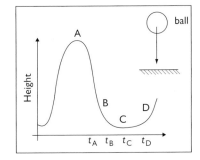

12 At the battle of Agincourt in 1415, the English archers overcame a much stronger French army by shooting arrows from longbows which required a maximum force of about 800 N to draw the string back a distance of half a metre. The graph shows the force–extension graph for a helical spring stretched elastically through this distance by this force.

Calculate the energy stored in the spring for an extension of half a metre. [2]

The arrows used at Agincourt were able to penetrate light armour and had a mass of about 60 g. Use your calculated value of energy to find an approximate value for the speed at which the arrow would leave the bow. [3]

In practice, the energy stored in the drawn bow is more than that stored in the helical spring stretched the same amount by the same force. Add, to a copy of the spring's graph, a possible force–extension graph for this bow. [2]

The arrows were fired upwards at an angle of 45° to the horizontal. Describe and explain what happens during the flight to both the horizontal and the vertical velocity components. [2+3]

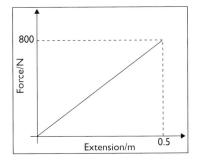

13 A mass of 100 g is dropped at time $t = 0$. The graph shows its kinetic energy W at times from 0 to 2.5 s.

Use the graph to find the rate of increase of kinetic energy of the mass at time $t = 2.0$ s. Explain your method. [3]

How much energy is transferred to the body during the second second? [2]

Explain why the energy transferred to the body during the second second is greater than the energy transferred to the body during the first second, even though the force acting on the body is constant. [3]

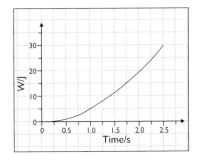

14 For each of the statements below state whether it is true or false.

(a) The gradient of a displacement–time curve is the acceleration at that instant.

(b) The acceleration of a ball which is thrown upwards is a maximum at the instant the ball changes direction.

(c) For a body to move at constant speed along a circular path, the centripetal force must be constant.

(d) An equation which is homogeneous must be correct.

15 A body of mass m is moving with constant speed v along a horizontal circular path of radius r. It has acceleration of magnitude v^2/r and direction towards the centre of the circular path.

Show that the expression v^2/r has the same units as acceleration. [2]

How can the velocity of the mass vary while its speed is constant? [2]

EXAMINATION QUESTIONS

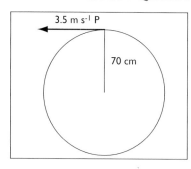

16 A stone of mass 150 g moves in a vertical circle on the end of a length of string. The radius of the circle is 70 cm and the speed of the stone at the topmost point P is 3.5 m s^{-1}.

Sketch and label a free-body force diagram for the stone for the instant at which the stone passes the point P. [2]

Calculate the resultant force on the stone (i.e. the centripetal force) and the tension in the string when the stone is at point P. [2+3]

17 A copper wire is 2.0 m long and has a cross-sectional area of 1.0 mm^2. It has a potential difference of 0.12 V across it when the current in it is 3.5 A. Draw a circuit diagram to show how you would check these voltage and current values. [3]

Calculate the rate at which the power supply does work on the wire. [2]

Copper has about 1.7×10^{29} electrons per metre cubed. Calculate the drift speed of the charge carriers in the wire. [3]

The power from the supply connected to the wire is equal to the total force F_t on the electrons multiplied by the drift speed at which the electrons travel. Calculate F_t. [3]

18 A light-dependent resistor may be used with additional components to make a light meter. Sketch a diagram for a suitable circuit. [2]

Explain how your circuit works. [2]

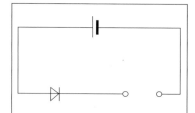

19 A cell of negligible internal resistance is connected in series with a microammeter of negligible resistance and two resistors of 10 kΩ and 15 kΩ. The current is 200 μA.

Draw a circuit diagram of the arrangement and calculate the e.m.f. of the cell. [1+2]

When a voltmeter is connected in parallel with the 15 kΩ resistor, the current in the microammeter increases to 250 μA. Sketch a diagram of the modified circuit and calculate the resistance of the voltmeter. [1+3]

20 Sketch and label two graphs to show how the current varies with potential difference for (i) a metal wire and (ii) a semiconductor diode, both being at a constant temperature. [2]

A semiconductor diode carries a current of 20 mA in normal operation. The potential difference across it should be 1.9 V. Copy and complete the diagram to show how, with the addition of a single component, the semiconductor diode may be powered from a 5 V supply. [1]

Calculate the value of the additional component required. [3]

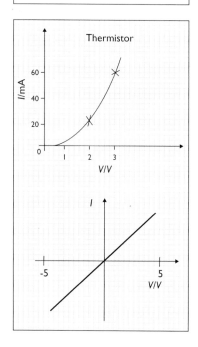

21 Define *electrical resistance*. [1]

The two graphs represent current–voltage characteristics for a metal conductor and a thermistor.

The resistance of the metal conductor is 833 Ω. What is the current through it when the voltage across it is 5 V? [3]

Calculate the change in resistance of the thermistor between the points A and B marked on the graph. [3]

What do the graphs tell you about the difference in behaviour between the metal and the thermistor? [2]

22 The battery in the circuit shown has an e.m.f. of 5.4 V and drives a current of 0.30 A through the lamp.

Copy the circuit diagram and label the voltmeter and the ammeter. [1]

The voltmeter reading is 4.8 V. Explain why the voltmeter reading is less than the e.m.f. of the battery. *cos it gets lost due to the wires* [2]

Calculate the internal resistance of the battery. [3]

Calculate the energy transformed each second in the lamp. [3]

State two assumptions you made in order to complete your calculations. [2]

23 The terminal potential difference of a cell is always less than the e.m.f. when there are 'lost volts' across the internal resistance. State a typical value for the e.m.f. of a single dry cell. State a typical value for the terminal potential difference for a dry cell supplying a normal load. Sketch a diagram to show how many such cells you would use, and how you would connect them, to provide a power supply for a 9 V radio. [3]

Some dry cells can cause serious burns if short-circuited by a bunch of keys while being carried in a pocket. Explain why this problem occurs only with cells like nickel–cadmium, which have a very low internal resistance. [3]

24 Define *capacitance*. [2]

An uncharged capacitor of 200 μF is connected in series with a 470 kΩ resistor, a 1.50 V cell and a switch. Draw a circuit diagram of this arrangement. Calculate the maximum current that flows. [1+2]

Sketch a graph of voltage against charge for this capacitor as it charges. Indicate on your graph the energy stored when the capacitor is fully charged. [4]

Calculate the energy stored in the fully charged capacitor. [2]

25 The potential difference between the plates of a 100 μF capacitor is 5.0 V. Calculate the charge and the energy stored in the capacitor. [2+2]

Describe how you would show by experiment that the charge stored in a 100 μF capacitor is proportional to the potential difference across the capacitor for the range of potential differences between 0 V and 10 V. [7]

26 Derive a formula for the equivalent capacitance of two capacitors in series. [4]

A 200 μF capacitor is connected in series with a 1000 μF capacitor and a battery of e.m.f. 9 V. Calculate the total capacitance, the charge that flows from the battery and the final potential difference across each capacitor. [2+2+3]

Things you need to know

Chapter 1

physical quantity: physical property that can be measured

base quantities: agreed minimum set of starting quantities for the system of measurement

derived quantity: quantity derived from combinations of base quantities

unit: agreed quantity, used for comparing other quantities

base unit: unit for a base quantity

derived unit: unit for a derived quantity

homogeneous: of the same type; correct equations must be homogeneous, but homogeneous equations need not be correct

Chapter 2

displacement: distance moved in a particular direction

scalar: quantity having size only and no direction

vector: quantity having size and direction

speed: distance/time; a scalar quantity

average speed: total distance/total time

velocity: displacement/time; a vector quantity

acceleration: change in velocity/time; a vector quantity

rate of: divided by time

Chapter 3

gradient of displacement–time graph: (instantaneous) velocity

gradient of velocity–time graph: (instantaneous) acceleration

area under velocity–time graph: change in displacement

Chapter 5

projectile motion: horizontal and vertical motions are independent of each other; horizontal velocity constant if air resistance is ignored; vertically the body accelerates downwards all the time

Chapter 6

force: something that can cause a body to accelerate; a vector quantity

resultant force: single force that could replace all other forces and have the same effect

equilibrium: condition where resultant force is zero and any forces acting are balanced

Newton I: a body will remain at rest or continue to move with a constant velocity as long as the forces on it are balanced

inertia: reluctance of a body to change its velocity

Chapter 7

one newton: the resultant force that will give a mass of 1 kg an acceleration of 1 m s^{-2}

Newton II: acceleration of a body is proportional to the resultant force and takes place in the direction of the force

Chapter 8

Newton III: while body A exerts a force on body B, body B exerts an equal and opposite force on body A

Chapter 9

weight: gravitational force on a body

contact forces: electrostatic forces between the outer layers of electrons of the bodies in contact

Chapter 10

Newton III force pairs: equal magnitude and opposite direction; act on different bodies for the same length of time; same type of force and line of action

Chapter 11

component: effect of a vector in a particular direction; magnitude = force × cosine of angle between original and required direction

Chapter 12

tangential force: force that acts along a surface

drag: force that opposes relative motion in a fluid

Chapter 13

tension: state caused by forces that stretch an object

compression: state caused by forces that squash an object

couple: pair of equal and opposite parallel forces that are not in line and produce a rotational effect

moment of a force: force × perpendicular distance from a point

moment of a couple: one of the forces × perpendicular distance between them

torque: turning moment of a set of forces that tend to cause rotation

principle of moments: if a body is in equilibrium, the sum of the moments about any axis must be zero

centre of gravity (mass): point where all the weight of the body appears to act

Chapter 15

momentum: mass × velocity

conservation of momentum: provided no external forces act, the total momentum in any direction remains constant

Chapter 16

Newton II: rate of change of momentum of a body is directly proportional to the resultant force acting on it and takes place in the same direction as the resultant force

force: quantity which causes a rate of change of momentum

impulse: force × time; area under force–time graph; equal to change of momentum

Chapter 17

system: any body or group of bodies under consideration

work: force × distance moved in the direction of the force; area under force–displacement graph; equal to the energy transferred from one system to another

power: rate of doing work: force × velocity; watt = joule/second

Chapter 18

gravitational potential energy: energy associated with position in a gravitational force; change = $mg\Delta h$

kinetic energy: energy associated with the motion of a body = $\frac{1}{2}mv^2$

Chapter 19

internal energy: random kinetic and potential energy of the molecules of a body

conservation of energy: energy content of a closed or isolated system remains constant

efficiency: useful energy output/total energy input

Chapter 20

elastic collision: one in which kinetic energy is conserved

inelastic collision: one in which kinetic energy is not conserved

THINGS YOU NEED TO KNOW

Chapter 21

radian: central angle where arc length = radius

centripetal acceleration: acceleration of a body following a circular path; directed towards centre of circle

centripetal force: resultant force that has to acts towards the centre of a circle to make a body follow a circular path

period: time for one complete rotation

frequency: number of complete rotations each second

angular velocity: rate at which central angle changes each second

Chapter 22

weightless: having no weight

apparent weightlessness: situation that occurs when a body is in free fall; the only force on the body is its weight.

Chapter 23

charge carrier: something that moves in a circuit to make a current

current: a flow of charge

cell: device for supplying electricity from two electrodes placed in chemicals

battery: collection of cells connected together

Chapter 24

charge: quantity associated with electrical forces; like charges repel, and unlike charges attract

neutral: having an equal number of positive and negative charges resulting in no overall electrical effects

coulomb: unit of charge; equal to an amp second

current: rate of flow of charge; amp = coulomb per second

Chapter 25

shunt: device added in parallel with an ammeter to increase its range

series: components connected so that current goes through one and then through the next and then through the next in turn

Chapter 26

(charge) carrier density: number of charged particles per metre cubed that are free to move and carry current

drift speed: average rate of progress of the carriers through a circuit; very slow

Chapter 27

resistor: component that opposes the flow of current

light-dependent resistor: resistance decreases as level of illumination increases

thermistor: resistance which changes as the temperature changes

parallel: components connected across each other; the voltage across each is the same; the current has a choice of routes

Kirchhoff I: the sum of the currents entering a point is equal to the sum of the currents leaving that point

Chapter 29

electromotive force: voltage across a component, such as a cell or a generator, that does work on a charge

potential difference: voltage across a component, such as a resistor or a lamp, that takes energy from a charge

voltage: work done moving a unit charge; measured with reference to two points; volt = joule per coulomb

Chapter 31

voltage at a point: voltage difference between zero (0 V) and that point

voltage across a component: difference between the voltage at one end and the voltage at the other end

Kirchhoff II: around any closed loop, the sum of the e.m.f.s is equal to the sum of the p.d.s

Chapter 32

resistance: property of a *component* that opposes current

Chapter 33

resistivity: property of a *material* which shows how well it conducts

metals: have high carrier density; reduction of drift velocity with increasing temperature decreases current flow

semiconductors: have low carrier density, which increases with increasing temperature allowing greater current flow despite reduction of drift speed with temperature

Chapter 34

potential divider: chain of resistors that divides up the voltage from a source in proportion to the resistance values

Chapter 35

rheostat: variable resistor, connected in series with component, to control the current through it

potentiometer: variable potential divider used to control the voltage across a component

V–I characteristics: graph showing how current varies with voltage

Ohm's law: current through component is proportional to voltage across provided the temperature remains constant

ohmic: component that obeys Ohm's law: *V–I* characteristics show a straight line through the origin

diode: component that conducts easily in one (forward) direction but not in the other (reverse)

forward direction: current flows freely in this direction through a diode

reverse direction: very little current flows in this direction through a diode

Chapter 36

terminal p.d.: voltage across terminals of a supply; work done on external circuit per coulomb of charge that flows

lost volts: difference between e.m.f. and terminal p.d.; voltage across internal resistance of supply

internal resistance: resistance to flow of current within power supply

e.m.f.: work done by supply on both external and internal resistances per coulomb of charge that flows

Chapter 37

capacitor: electrical device used to store energy by means of a displacement of charge within it

Chapter 38

capacitance: the ability of a component to 'store' charge; farad = coulomb per volt

Equations to learn

Weight	$W = mg$
Velocity	$v = dx/dt$
Acceleration	$a = dv/dt$
Momentum	$p = mv$
Force	$F = ma$
Work done	$\Delta W = F\Delta x$
Power	$P = \Delta W/\Delta T = \Delta E/\Delta t$
Kinetic energy	k.e. $= \frac{1}{2}\Delta mv$
Gravitational potential energy	$W = mg/\Delta h$ (close to the Earth)
Centripetal force	$F = mv^2/r$
Moment of *F* about O	$= F \times$ (Perpendicular distance from O to *F*)
Sum of clockwise moment about any point in a plane	= sum of anticlockwise moments about that point
Electric current	$I = dQ/dt$
Electric energy transferred	$W = IVt$
Potential difference	$V = W/Q$
Resistance	$R = V/I = pl/A$
Capacitance	$C = Q/V$

Index

Page references in italics refer to a table or an illustration.

INDEX